Francesca Woodman

On Being an Angel

Francesca Woodman

On Being an Angel

MODERNA MUSEET

Verlag der Buchhandlung Walther und Franz König

Contents

Foreword

"Then at one point I did not need to translate the notes; they went directly to my hands"

Francesca Woodman wrote these words in the lower corner of a photograph from 1976. It shows her hands feeling their way up a wall as she squats down with her back to the camera, her body hidden behind a strip of wallpaper. Francesca Woodman may only have been a teenager when she composed this image, but she was, even then, already an artist poised to make history.

In the exhibition at Moderna Museet, this photograph is among the one 102 images on display, complemented by an early video work. Francesca Woodman often used her body as a starting point, acting both as object and subject, and excavating a new role for the artist in still photography. There is a kind of movement in her aesthetic world, in which the surroundings, the room, objects, and her own body are arranged in remarkable constellations and are subjected to her investigative gaze. She often appended her images with a handwritten comment, placing these scenes in yet another sphere.

Moderna Museet is delighted and proud to finally be able to present Woodman's unique and spectacular artistry so comprehensively. The museum's curator of photography, Anna Tellgren, has approached this project with great sensitivity and a deep understanding of Francesca Woodman's significance in the history of contemporary art and photography. We offer her our warmest thanks for this and for her erudite text in this catalog. The exhibition would not have been possible without the abundant support offered by the artist's parents, Betty and George Woodman. The importance of the family's engagement and the generosity of The Estate of Francesca Woodman, along with that of Katarina Jerinic, who provided us with materials and information, cannot be underscored enough. We would like to extend especial gratitude to George Woodman for his insightful contribution to this catalog, which highlights the movement in his daughter's pioneering photography. In her essay, the author Anna-Karin Palm explores how the body in Francesca Woodman's photographs both carries the narrative and drives it forward – thank you very much for this wonderful text! Further thanks are owed to the designer of the catalog, Patric Leo, and to the museum's managing editor, Teresa Hahr, whose steady hand has guided the catalog from its inception to print.

The exhibition will be shown in Stockholm in the autumn of 2015. It will then tour Amsterdam and Paris in the winter and spring of 2016, before traveling to Moderna Museet Malmö. Collaborating with some of Europe's most significant photography institutions has been a sincere pleasure. Special thanks are due to Marloes Krijnen, founding director of the Foam Photography Museum, and to Agnès Sire, director of the Fondation Henri Cartier-Bresson. Together with our partners in Amsterdam and Paris, we invite the public in each of these countries to experience one of our most important contemporary artists. Welcome!

Daniel Birnbaum, Director
Ann-Sofi Noring, Co-Director

Francesca Woodman

On Being an Angel

ANNA TELLGREN

Throughout her career, the young American photographer Francesca Woodman revisited the theme of angels. In *On Being an Angel* (1976), she is seen bending backward as light falls on her white body. A black umbrella is in the distance. The following year she made a new version – an image with a darker mood in which she shows her face. Woodman developed the angel motif during a visit to Rome, where she photographed herself in a large, abandoned building. In these images, she is wearing a white petticoat, but her chest is bare. White pieces of cloth in the background are like wings. She called these photographs *From Angel series* (1977) and *From a series on Angels* (1977). There are also a number of pictures simply called *Angels* (1977–78), and among them is one where again she is bending backward, but this time in front of a graffitied wall. These angels are but a few examples of Francesca Woodman's practice of staging her body and her face. In the few intense years before her far too premature passing, she created a collection of fascinating photographs. Her body of work has been the subject of many in-depth studies and large exhibitions, and her photography has inspired generations of artists and photographers around the world.

Francesca Woodman was born into a family of artists in Denver, Colorado, on April 3, 1958. Her mother, Betty, was a sculptor, her father, George, a painter and photographer, and her brother, Charlie, was a video artist. The family often traveled to Italy and lived in Florence for a year between 1965 and 1966. Then they returned home to Boulder, Colorado, and Francesca continued her schooling. In 1968 her parents bought a farmhouse outside of Florence in Antella, and there they would spend their summers. Italy and its language, culture, and art history were frequent sources of inspiration for Francesca Woodman.

Woodman started taking pictures as a teenager and had attended a few art courses before she moved to Providence to study at the Rhode Island School of Design (RISD) in 1975. The college is among the oldest art schools in the United States, and the well-known photographer Aaron Siskind was one of her teachers. While at college, she lived in her studio in an industrial area where many of her pictures from that time were created. Between 1977 and 1978 Francesca Woodman spent a year in Rome as part of the school's honors program. In the fall of 1978, she earned her BFA and exhibited the series *Swan Song* (1978) at the graduate show in RISD's Woods-Gerry Gallery.

Months later, in January 1979, Woodman moved to New York, where she lived at various addresses while looking for work. She spent the summer together with her boyfriend, Benjamin Moore, in Stanwood, Washington. Over the course of the next year, she exhibited her work at a number of smaller galleries and experimented with new techniques such as large-format diazotypes, and color images. She was a fellow at the MacDowell Colony in Peterborough, New Hampshire, in the summer of 1980. There, she worked on a series of images exploring the relationship between nature and her body, among other projects. In early 1981, her artist's book *Some Disordered Interior Geometries* was published by Synapse Press in Philadelphia. This was one of seven notebooks (including photographs that were glued in) that she worked with from 1976 onwards. Francesca Woodman took her own life on January 19, 1981.

Francesca Woodman's work is usually split into five periods: the early works, her years at RISD, in Italy, at the MacDowell Colony, and finally her time in New York from 1979 until her death. Analysis of her work is often linked to her biography and chronology. During her active years, Woodman produced thousands of images. Around eight hundred photographs are preserved by The Estate of Francesca Woodman in New York. She scrawled words, short sentences, or quotations on many of her prints, and these jottings have since given those pieces their titles. Woodman sometimes wrote letters on her photographs and mailed them to family and friends. Collections of her letters have been published, and along with her notes these inform most of what we know about her processes and ideas. In addition to her parents, close friends, former classmates, and teachers, people who met or lived with her have been important sources of information. Because she gave away or sent off many of her photographs, it's difficult to know exactly how many of Francesca Woodman's vintage prints have been preserved. Significant collections of her photographs can be found at the Metropolitan Museum in New York, Tate Modern in London, and the Sammlung Verbund in Vienna, for example.

This exhibition is comprised of one hundred and two photographs and one video by Francesca Woodman, and selections from most of her thematic groups and series are represented. She often obscured her subject by placing her models behind furniture and other interior design elements or by blurring the image. Her themes are intimate – a feeling that is heightened by the small format of many of her images. Woodman often worked in unusual environments, such as derelict buildings, and she liked to make use of mirrors and glass, which creates a surreal and sometimes claustrophobic mood. In *Space²* (1976), she used a large glass vitrine, the kind you find in museums; inside it, a seated person presses her body against the glass. In another version, Woodman has placed the skeleton of an animal in the case, and her face appears behind it. This theme is further developed in *From Space²* (1976), which shows her covered by the wallpaper in the room.

The notion of transformation also emerges in one of Woodman's strongest and eeriest series, *House,* from 1976, in which she gradually disappears into the walls, the torn wallpaper, the open fireplace, and other interior elements. And in the *Polka Dots* series (1976) the model, Francesca Woodman, becomes a part of the wall or the house. In a self-portrait from 1976, she squats in the corner of her studio. She wears a wrinkled dress (or perhaps it's a silk robe) and meets our gaze. Light spills through the large windows. This slightly overexposed picture is beautiful and mysterious. It's as if she could vanish from the room, out of the picture, at any given second. This idea of transformation is expanded upon in a work from the summer of 1980 – her arms are covered in bark, and she is becoming part of the tree and of nature. There is an allusion here to Daphne: a nymph in Greek mythology who was transformed into a laurel tree to escape Apollo's amorous pursuit of her. In this and other images from the MacDowell Colony, Woodman experimented with a technique that involved placing several negatives on the photographic paper at once, like a contact sheet, thereby creating a sort of collage.

Francesca Woodman's consistent use of the female form as a starting point for her photographs – as a surface on which we can project our gazes and desires – has inspired feminist interpretations and attempts to locate her in that tradition. One of the most important critical contributions was made by the art historian and feminist Abigail Solomon-Godeau. Her text was published in Woodman's first exhibition catalog, from 1986. In a later study from 2014, Solomon-Godeau develops and comments on her first encounter with Woodman's photographs, but in the earlier text, she had already addressed the themes that would go on to be revisited by many other writers. Solomon-Godeau asserts that we can't know if Woodman had knowledge of or any relationship to contemporary feminist theories, but her preoccupation with the body, the dichotomy of subject–object, and female iconography encourage a feminist reading. Among a number of insightful observations and analyses, she points out that Woodman's seemingly traditional nudes (with reference to art history) often include a detail that disrupts the composition and forces us to consider them more deeply. One example is *Untitled* (1979–80). A naked woman is lying across a Victorian sofa. On closer inspection, we see that she is wearing several garter belts. The extra stockings adorn the wall behind the sofa, inviting various interpretations. On the point of multiple meanings and complexity in Woodman's work, Solomon-Godeau references one photograph from *Three kinds of melon in four kinds of light series* (1976), and she provides one possible reading of it. Woodman has photographed a woman sitting at a table. The picture is cropped so we can only see her bare breasts and two halves of a melon on the table. The woman is holding a postcard featuring a painting of a melon in front of one of her breasts. Of course, comparing breasts to melons is a conventional metaphor. The graphic representation, the drawing, appears in several of Woodman's compositions and could be an expression of the patriarchal order in which women are carriers of meaning, rather than creators of meaning. This photograph is the last in a series of four. The woman in the picture was Woodman's neighbor in Providence, and we can tell that she is pregnant, which suggests that this in fact could be what Woodman is referring to in the title.

In *Charlie the Model* (1976–77), Francesca Woodman enlisted Charlie, who had worked for many years as a model at RISD. This series is one of the few that features a male figure. Charlie was photographed sitting or standing in a corner of the studio and with various objects: a piece of paper, a mirror, and a glass bowl. Eventually, the artist herself appears in the composition and they play in front of the camera. Finally, Charlie sits on the floor with a plate of glass pressed against his body, and everything takes a slightly unexpected turn when we read what Woodman wrote on the photograph that Charlie had a heart attack. The mirror and the plate of glass are motifs that also appear in several other series.

In Woodman's active years in the late 1970s and early 1980s, photography was in a period of transition. Many photographers who had worked with classic black-and-white photography were experimenting with other forms and were pushing the documentary tradition toward more subjective and surrealist projects. The United States paved the way in this development, and when many curators, gallerists, editors, and critics started working more professionally with photography, it was institutionalized. This shift in the field eventually spread to Europe. Major photographic exhibitions were held at The Museum of Modern Art in New York, featuring artists such as

Diane Arbus, Robert Frank, Lee Friedlander, and William Eggleston, all of whom were influential to many younger photographers and to the articulation of the medium's aesthetic potential. *New Topographics. Photographs of a Man-Altered Landscape* (1975) was another significant exhibition. It was held at the International Museum of Photography at George Eastman House in Rochester and one of the featured artists was Lewis Baltz. Other notable photographers in the new American wave were personalities as diverse as Ralph Gibson, Kenneth Josephson, Robert Mapplethorpe, Duane Michals, Melissa Shook, Arthur Tress, and Jerry Uelsmann. But it was also then, from 1977 forward, that Cindy Sherman started working on her break-out series *Untitled Film Stills.* Sherman is an artist of the post-modern generation, and it is not known if Woodman had been aware of the so-called Pictures Generation. Duane Michals was one of the photographers who we know interested Woodman. Michals stood for a more conceptual approach to the creation of images, investigating the intangibles of human existence in his picture-stories. His photographs often feature handwritten, poetic texts with dictums on death, dreams, homosexuality, and the cosmos.

Francesca Woodman used this approach in three pictures from her university days in Providence, for instance. Continuing the house series, one image shows her squatting, turned toward a wall, and covered with wallpaper. On the picture are the words: "Then at one point I did not need to translate the notes; they went directly to my hands." Woodman had played the piano during her childhood. Music, or rather practicing playing music, is a theme that returns in a 1977 image of a woman wearing a loose black dress, likely the artist herself. The image is cropped at the neck. She holds a fruit knife in her right hand. The low neckline exposes one breast, bleeding photographs in the form of strips of contact sheets. At the bottom, Woodman has written "I could no longer play I could not play by instinct." In another portrait, she poses with her hand under her breast, as if to present it, and there it says: "And I had forgotten how to read music." In an essay from 1998, her friend Sloan Rankin states that the quotation is taken from a longer poem that Woodman had written in their first year of college. In seven stanzas, she describes her worry about and her experiences of playing. Writing and drawing seem to have been a way for her to work things through and to remember, testing ideas and notions before embarking on photographic projects.

Woodman's aesthetic world clearly references Surrealism, and this aspect has been addressed in many readings of her work. There are similarities in style to surrealistic photography, such as Woodman's frequent use of mirrors, doubles, shadows, gloves, hands, swans, fish, eels, masks, and sexual symbols. Photographers such as Hans Bellmer, Claude Cahun, and Man Ray spring to mind. During her residency in Rome, Woodman connected with the owners of the Libreria Maldoror – a bookshop specialized in historical avant-garde and surrealist literature, as well as a meeting place for artists, which she'd visit on her way from her apartment in Rome to the school in the Palazzo Cenci. There, she found old notebooks from the 1930s, anonymous postcards and other items that she would later use in her work. She read André Breton's 1928 novel, *Nadja*, and other surrealist texts. They also had a gallery in the basement for smaller exhibitions, and Woodman exhibited her photographs there in March 1978. During this period she also worked on the angel series, a collection of still lifes featuring birds, and *Self-deceit* (1978): a series of seven photographs showing an interplay between a mirror and her naked body in which they become one with each other and the room's stark walls and floors.

There's a kind of movement in many of Francesca Woodman's photographs. She often worked with series, and blurriness was one way of creating a sense of time and motion in still images. In *Untitled* (1977–78), she is shown mid-jump; it's as if she's lifting herself up from the floor by her hair. Her many angel images also suggest movement and the ability to fly. It's only a small leap from these images to actual moving pictures, and while at RISD, Woodman also attended lectures at the fairly new video course at the school. *Selected Video Works* (1976–78), edited in 2004 and published by The Estate of Francesca Woodman, is a collection of six short videos. In the 2011 catalog, Jennifer Blessing conducts a deep analysis of these works and writes about how seeing the first video in particular is like watching one of Woodman's photographs come to life. In this film, Francesca Woodman stands in the nude behind a large sheet of paper and slowly writes her name on it. Again, she uses her body and lets it occupy the room and the frame through the camera. Seeing her move and hearing her voice is an incredibly emotional experience – as viewers, this piece offers us a proximity to her process that is different to what can be sensed through her still images. A number of themes in these videos overlap with those explored in her photographs: sculptures and bodies, corners of rooms, traces and silhouettes, along with masks on or off of the artist's face.

When Francesca Woodman moved to New York, she had several short-term jobs as a secretary, a photographer's assistant, and a model.

She needed to find a way to support herself and tried fashion photography. One of her role models was the American fashion photographer Deborah Turbeville, who is renowned for her intimate and romantic style. Among these works are some of Woodman's rare color photographs – a series of eight that shifts from mint green to pale pink to cream and orange. Through her job as an assistant, Woodman met several models she would later use in her own explorations of the genre. Her images, however, were never published in fashion magazines. There are other studies from this time in which she used models, clothing, jewelry, and mirrors, elements that recall props in her fashion photography, but which are more at home in her artistic projects. This fascinating overlap between Woodman's commercial and creative projects shows how her ideas for images moved across her practice.

In the spring of 1980 Francesca Woodman started working on *Blueprint for a Temple*. It could be said that she was recreating the facade of a Greek temple using models draped in tunics similar to caryatids. The series began with a collection of details from bathrooms in New York, reminiscent of classical motifs. From having worked on a smaller scale, she had now moved on to truly large formats, some several meters in size. These pictures are often categorized as blueprints, referring to a method of reproduction most frequently used for architectural plans. This is a contact print process on photosensitive paper; white lines on a blue background distinguish the finished product. (Other types of paper produced different background colors.) The technique Woodman used was diazotypy: a dry photographic process on paper coated with diazonium compounds, which are sensitive to blue and UV light and developed by ammonia vapour. Woodman experimented with this technique. She created the largest of these images by hanging a long sheet of photosensitive diazo paper on the wall of a darkroom. A photographic slide was projected onto the paper from a slide projector, often for hours. The paper was then developed in a diazo processor at a company that made commercial reproductions of architectural plans. The result was a set of magnificent works in blue, purple, and sepia tones. In the long and narrow *Zig Zag Study* (1980), Woodman brought together several motifs, such as feet, legs, arms, and plants, piecing them together to create a zigzag pattern. Formal aspects take prominence in several of these works. *Head on Rug* (1980), a brown-toned image in three parts, shows a woman lying in the center of an oriental rug. In the right-hand field, a white lily has been placed next to the floral rug, creating an interplay between perspective and the planes of the image.

The first major retrospective of Francesca Woodman's work was produced in 1986 by Ann Gabhart in collaboration with Rosalind Krauss for the Wellesley College Museum. It then toured a number of museums at American universities. Her first European exhibition was held in 1992 by Shedhalle in Zurich and the Westfälischer Kunstverein in Münster and was shown in the spring of 1993 at The Finnish Museum of Photography, in the Cable Factory in Helsinki. On its way there, it stopped for two months at Kulturhuset in Stockholm. The critic Lars O Ericsson wrote in *Dagens Nyheter* that the exhibition may have been the most important one to see in the capital at the time. To date, at least fifty separate exhibitions of Woodman's photography have been held in Europe and the United States.

Francesca Woodman's youth is mentioned in nearly every text about her, and in the retelling of nearly every memory. How could so young a person create such strong and complex images? She is described as unusually talented and as a prodigy. Those who met her testify to her as a young woman who was always working and looking for subjects and material for her photographs. She often found clever and witty solutions to her images. Though a large part of her oeuvre is comprised of work from her time at college in Providence, we are engaging with extremely mature artistry. To examine Francesca Woodman's aesthetic oeuvre is a challenge and an adventure. Her images reference history and the history of photography, but they also reflect their time while unlocking new interpretations. She is deeply personal, and so her themes become universal. All of this is what *On Being an Angel* is about.

The Body and Its Stories

Thoughts on Francesca Woodman's Photography

ANNA-KARIN PALM

When I was young I moonlighted as an artist's model. The work was at once easy and demanding. Neither experience nor special knowledge was needed; that was the easy part. But other than it requiring a degree of courage to stand in the nude before a group of strangers who were all staring at my body, the job was physically demanding in a way that I couldn't have anticipated. How could standing still be so strenuous? Muscles I barely knew existed began to twitch and twinge, lactic acid rose through unknown channels, one arm felt as heavy as lead, and one leg was twisted in such a peculiar way that it felt like a foreign object. Is this my body? Is this me? The teacher spoke of highlights, volume, and lines. Just an object in the room, different techniques used to depict it. To this day I recall the unexpected, almost breathtaking liberation of being seen but not sexualized. To be so scrutinized, standing there being gazed upon by everyone with the anonymity of a thing. Invisibility in visibility. A body on a podium bathed in light. A task. An outstretched leg, toes touching the floor. Muscles and a skeleton and an overlay of skin. The peculiar freedom of this. The first time I saw Francesca Woodman's pictures, I recalled that strange, elating feeling of freedom.

*

A wall with two tall windows. A nude female body against the wall, partly concealed by large, loose sheets of floral wallpaper. The peeling paint, the cracks in the plaster, the scraps of wallpaper on the rough-hewn wooden floor. Her bare feet. Belly button. Hand holding the wallpaper covering her lower body, arm and stomach almost the same bleached white as the wall. Face hidden behind another strip of wallpaper. The sweeping cool light, the shades of gray on the wall. Is she hiding herself, about to coalesce with the wall and become part of the room? (The way wood nymphs could coalesce with tree trunks in an instant when the hunters neared.) Or is she about to emerge from the wall, peel away her layers of wallpaper, and step into the light? Take up space in the room. Take the space she needs.

(The picture is called *From Space*[2]. The word "space" could mean a place, an expanse or scope; to be heaven-sent, newly arrived; an alien or an angel. The body is also a place.)

*

We people say: I, and my body. One of the things that separates us from animals is that minute, momentary distance between *I* and *my body*. The body is the form to which we must relate and the vessel that carries us through life. The body is the house of the self, the dwelling of the soul. But the body can also be our prison and our burden. I, and my body. In between the two is a gap filled with riddles and secrets, darkness and promise. Out of that gap, or incision, or wound, grow songs and stories, religions, dreams, and discoveries.

And if the body is also a woman's body it's immediately more complicated because our culture has made the distance between body and soul so much greater and more difficult for women than for men. The corporeality of a man is the norm: a pure, sort of objective body free from complications. And man's subject, without much difficulty, seems to be able to enfold and also include his body. Woman has generally been associated more with the physical and with the reality of sex; the woman who seeks her soul and who insists on the right to be a unique subject will have to do battle with the body. For the body. For the right to be both I *and* my body. To be allowed to be the narrator.

The female body. Throughout the ages praised, depicted, described and elevated, pined for and idealized. But also turned into a taboo, regulated, dissected and analyzed, confined and used and subdued. By the male gaze, power, and narrating voice. There are so many stories about us and our bodies, but they are almost never told by us ourselves. How would it be interpreted, from within? The experience of living with, and in, this body. And not least: the experience of living with, and in, all the *ideas* about this body? This is a kind of fundamental research. I think it is extremely important.

*

The series *Self-deceit* is comprised of seven smaller pictures. One room, a naked woman, a broken mirror. The room is bare and worn, the plaster is flaking off the walls, the stone floor looks dirty, but the light is expansive.

Even though we see only sections of the room, it feels spacious, empty, and echoing. In the first image, the woman is crawling around a corner and catches sight of herself in the mirror, which is leaning against the wall. In the images that follow, the woman engages with the mirror in different ways. She lets it reflect the room, she turns her back to it, uses it to conceal herself, tries to crawl behind it. In picture #6 she sits with her back to the viewer, huddled next to the mirror right against the wall. Her head is tilted forward and so deeply cast in shadow that all we see is her pale back, as if this were a headless body, a torso stored in a corner. Pure form. The mirror is empty, reflecting only the distressed plaster wall on the other side of the room. Everything is bleached, bright, and very quiet. The dulled beauty of the blotches on the wall, the slim white back, the silvery mirror. An atmosphere of rest and petrification, of deep, muted melancholy. There is no way to be in that mirror, to be that mirrored image. You have to step out of the image, out of the self-deceit contained in that image. In the seventh and last picture this is exactly what happens. The woman has got up and is standing next to the mirror, but the focus has shifted away from her; it's now cutting into the sharp edges of the mirror, leaving the female body alone. The woman is in motion, her contours disappear into the pattern of the wall, half-dissolved, on her way out. It looks like she's stretching, with her arms over her head.

*

Francesca Woodman's photographs are the work of a young woman. There are some things a young person sees more clearly, when she hasn't yet grown accustomed to compromise and gray areas. Everything is more apparent, more sharply lit, feelings carved from the flesh. The sincere compass needles of questions through the body, those truly large questions that demand courage, intelligence, and an awakened presence in order to be asked. Fundamental research questions.

But those who think that by "a young woman's work" I mean something delicate or perhaps romantic think wrong. That which is striking and inspiring in Woodman's work is rather its power and richness of expression. It elates me, that power – raging, cheeky, playful, tender, dreamy, melancholic, defiant, humorous, aching, investigative, and lively. Woodman stages and narrates, she takes up space in a room. (Her pictures *take place*.) Also in time, her pictures are like shards of stories, they extend beyond the print, deep into the viewer. She aligns herself with the greater story that we call our cultural history through countless references to famous works, myths, and motifs, which she presents in her own way. (Lilies, the swan, snakes/eels, slender birch trunks, angel's wings – motifs that are connected to this matter of being a woman, of wearing a female body, and which in Woodman's interpretations become something entirely new and surprising.) It's not simple; there is great pain in this examination. Being honest with yourself often hurts, but it's the only way if you take your task seriously.

Woman and the female body are among the most common objects in art history. The man holds the brush and the woman allows herself to be depicted. Subject–object, active–passive, male–female. Oppositions such as these are like invisible yet influential gridlines across the history of art. A female artist must engage with this in some way. Can the dichotomy itself be disarmed? I think that's exactly what Francesca Woodman is doing. Paradoxically, by turning herself into her own object, Woodman is also the narrating subject. She uses her own body to stage an objectification, which is simultaneously invalidated by the fact that she is also the picture's subject, its guiding and gazing source. It's violently liberating!

*

A doorway leading into a room with a black-and-white patterned floor and high ceilings. In the center of the picture is an antique chair made of glossy dark wood, with a high back and carvings; a white cloth or an item of clothing has been tossed on the seat. A woman hangs in the doorway, wearing a loose-fitting, light-colored, wrinkled shirt. The light falls across her body and is concentrated on her bare legs and feet, blindingly white. A crucification motif, it's probably impossible to miss the association. The rich folds of the light-colored shirt over her arms are reminiscent of altarpieces and trompe l'oeils. Her face is half-hidden behind one arm, resting in humble shadow. The light on the glossy floorboards, on the white walls, and the floating white legs. Like with so many of Woodman's pictures, the many possible interpretations unlock one another, superimposed and layered. My initial interpretation is about the crucified woman, sacrificed and exposed in a world that largely still belongs to men, and where the female body to a terrifyingly large degree is still a commodity and the property of men. Then the next layer of interpretation arises – the crucified god, couldn't he be a she? One of our most potent and most dominant stories is staged here with a female protagonist; the son of man becomes a daughter, just as divine in her humble greatness. But then the picture's details start to creep up on me: the edge of a small round table in the corner, a sloppily coiled electrical cord along the baseboards, part of a poster on the wall. The light feels like morning, the white cloth on the chair is perhaps a robe, dropped in passing. Everyday details, a life in motion. And then it hits me: she's not crucified at all. The woman is hanging there in the doorway by her own might, held up by her own strong hands. As if she had jumped up impulsively. Muscles and sinews, light and shadow, heaviness and lightness. She's floating freely, hanging by her strong, straight arms, and maybe she is secretly smiling behind her left sleeve.

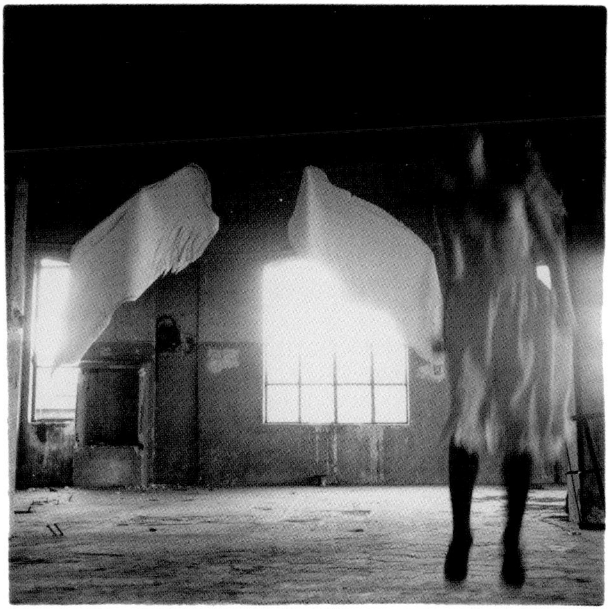

From Angel series, Rome, Italy, 1977

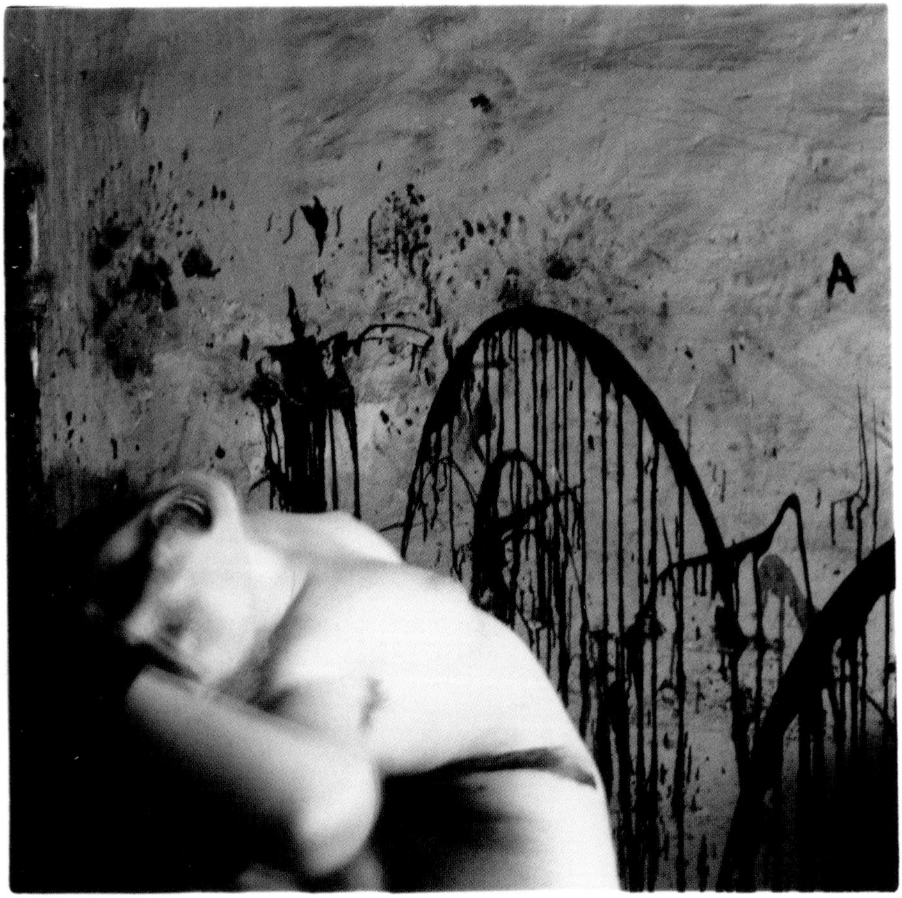

Angels, Italy, 1977–78

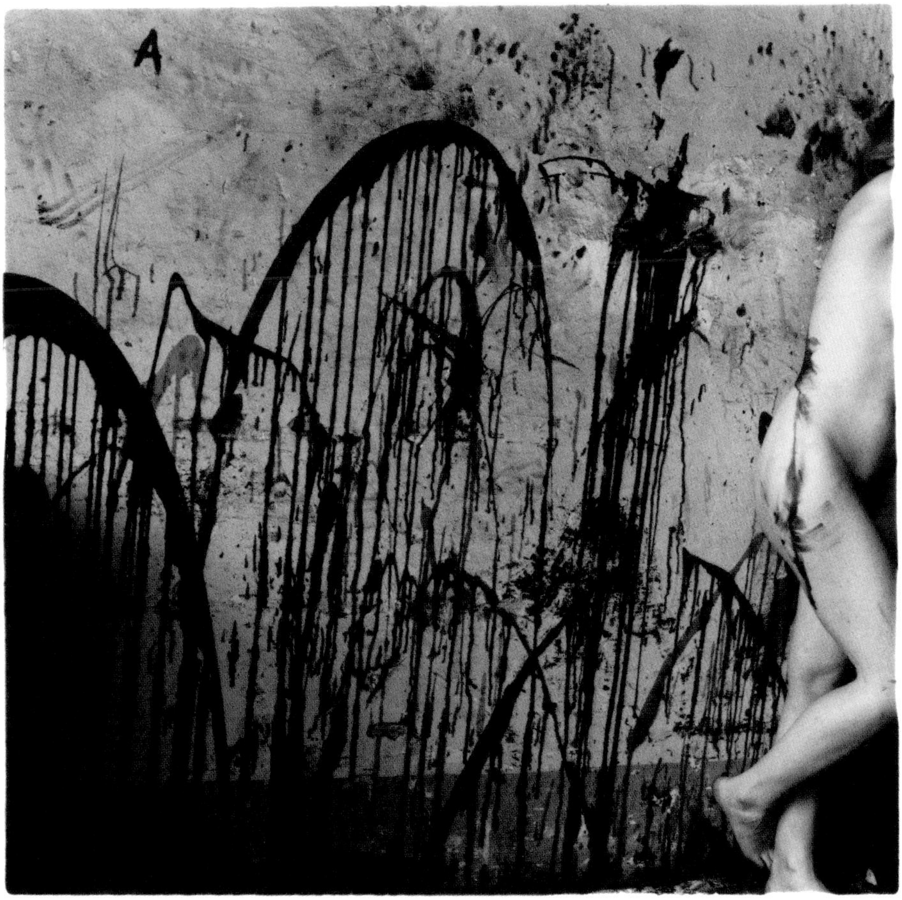

 Splatter Paint, Rome, Italy, 1977–78

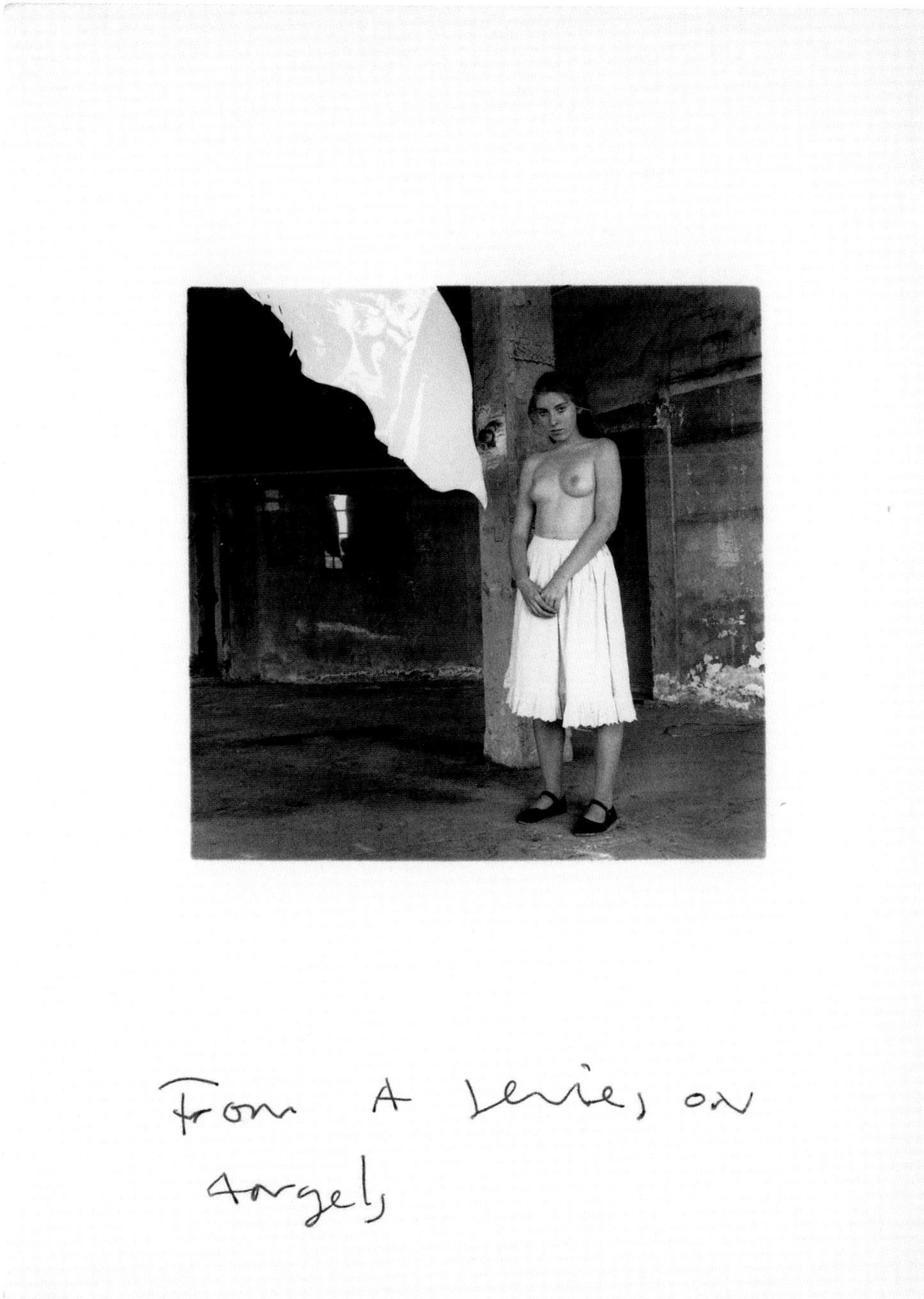

From a series on Angels, Rome, Italy, 1977

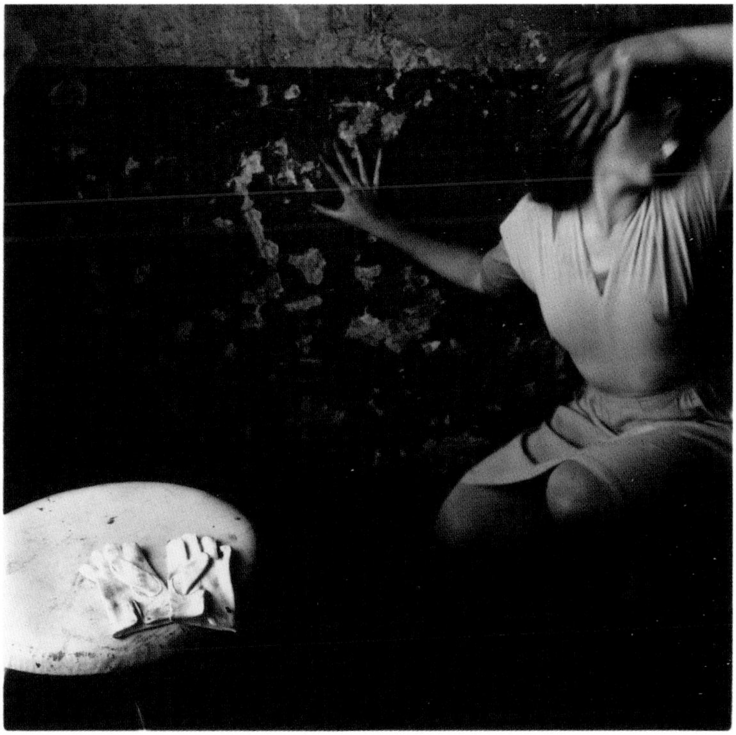

Angels, Italy, 1977–78

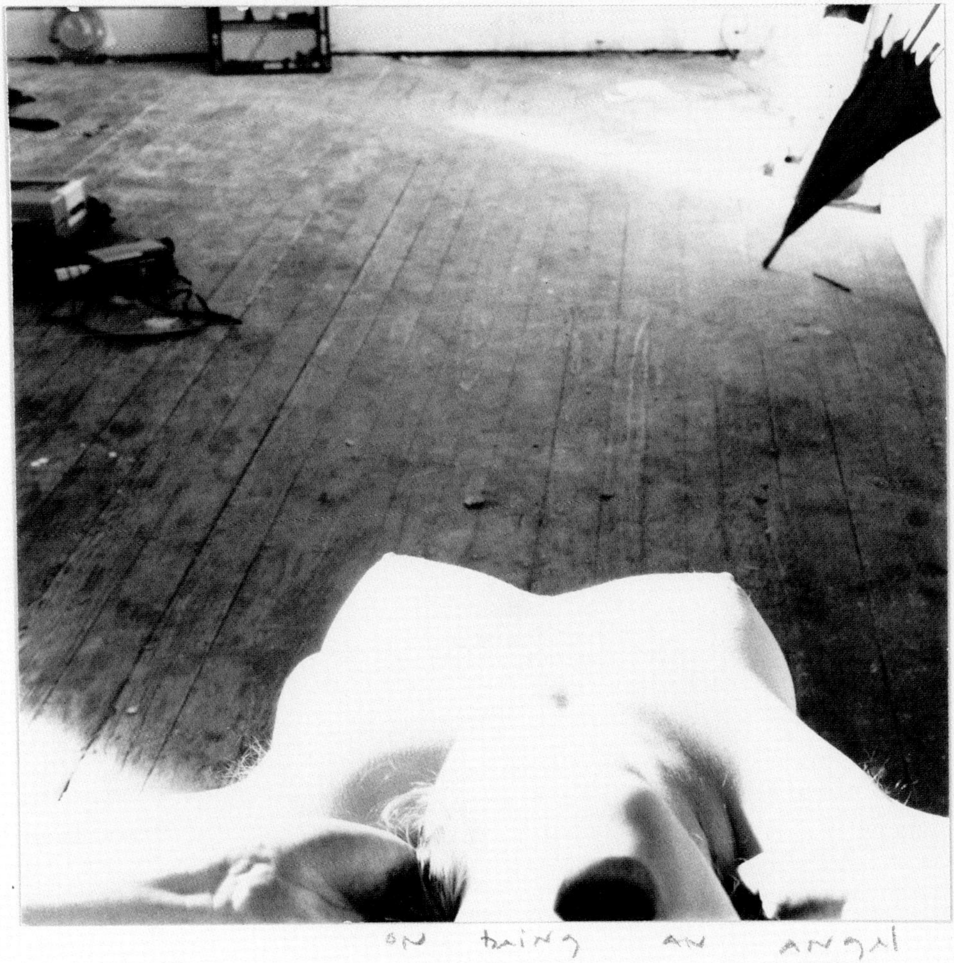

On Being an Angel, Providence, Rhode Island, 1976

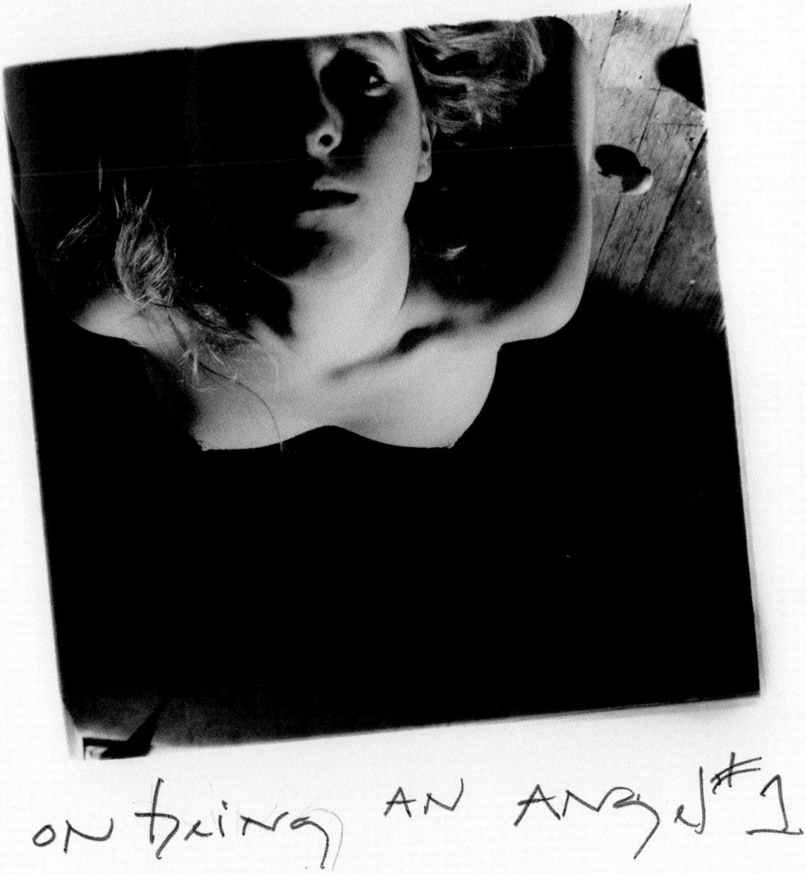

On Being an Angel #1, Providence, Rhode Island, 1977

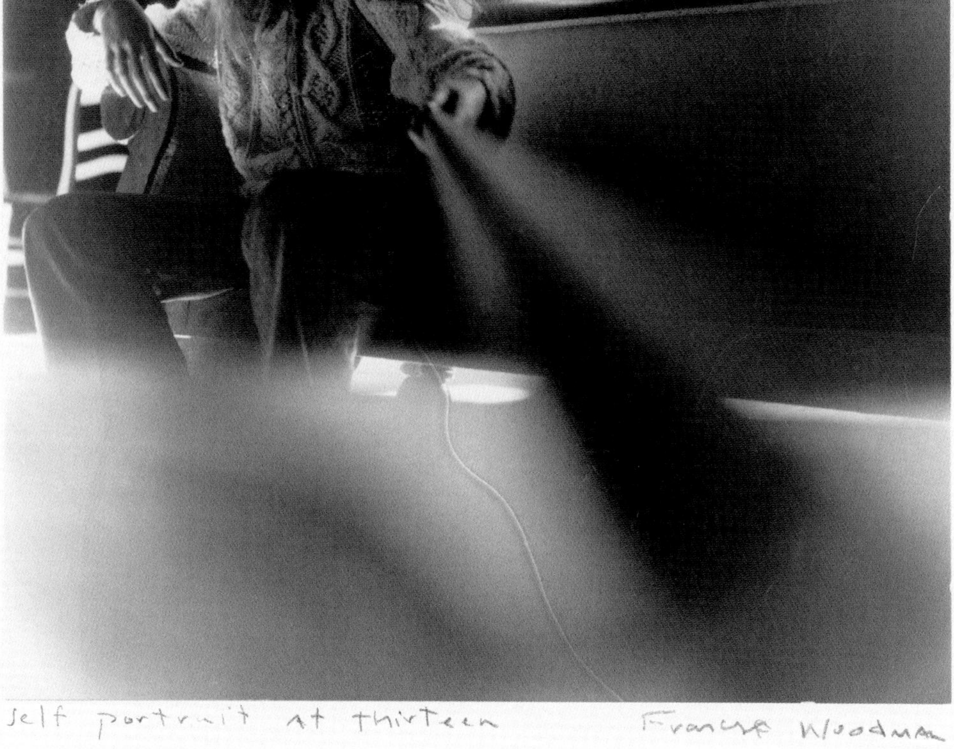

Self-portrait at thirteen, Antella, Italy, 1972

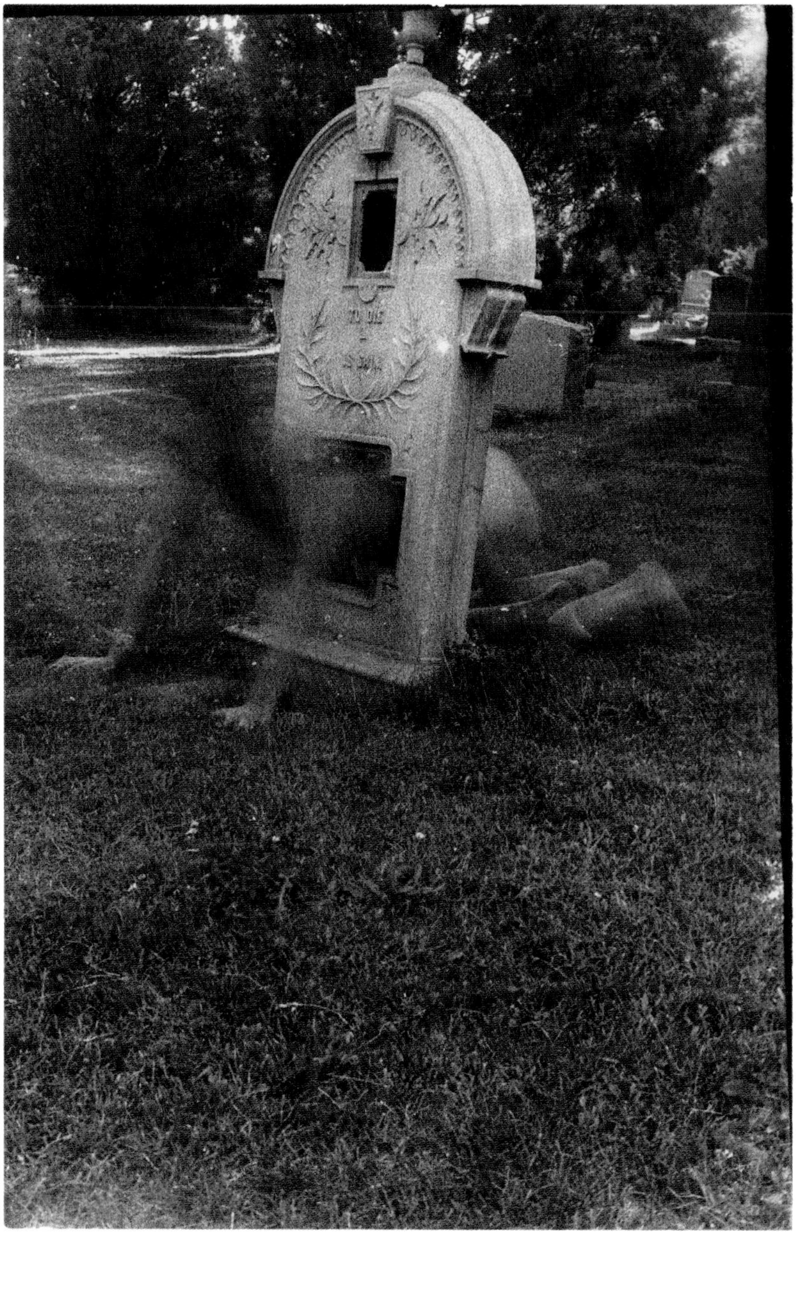

Untitled, Boulder, Colorado, 1972–75

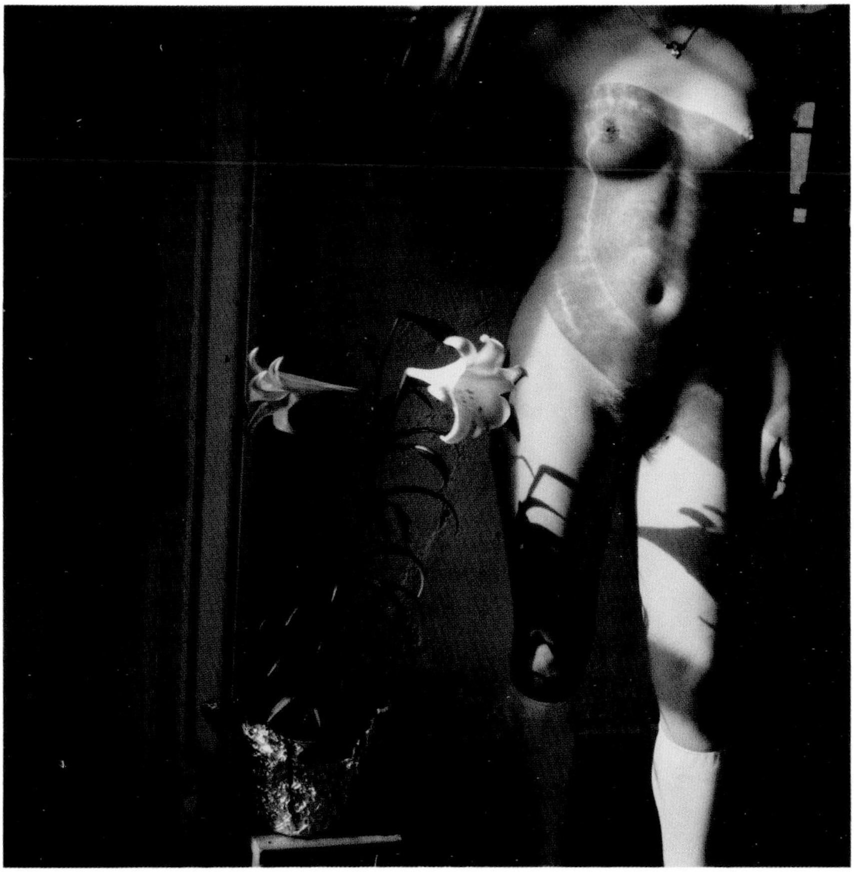

 Easter Lilies, Providence, Rhode Island, 1976

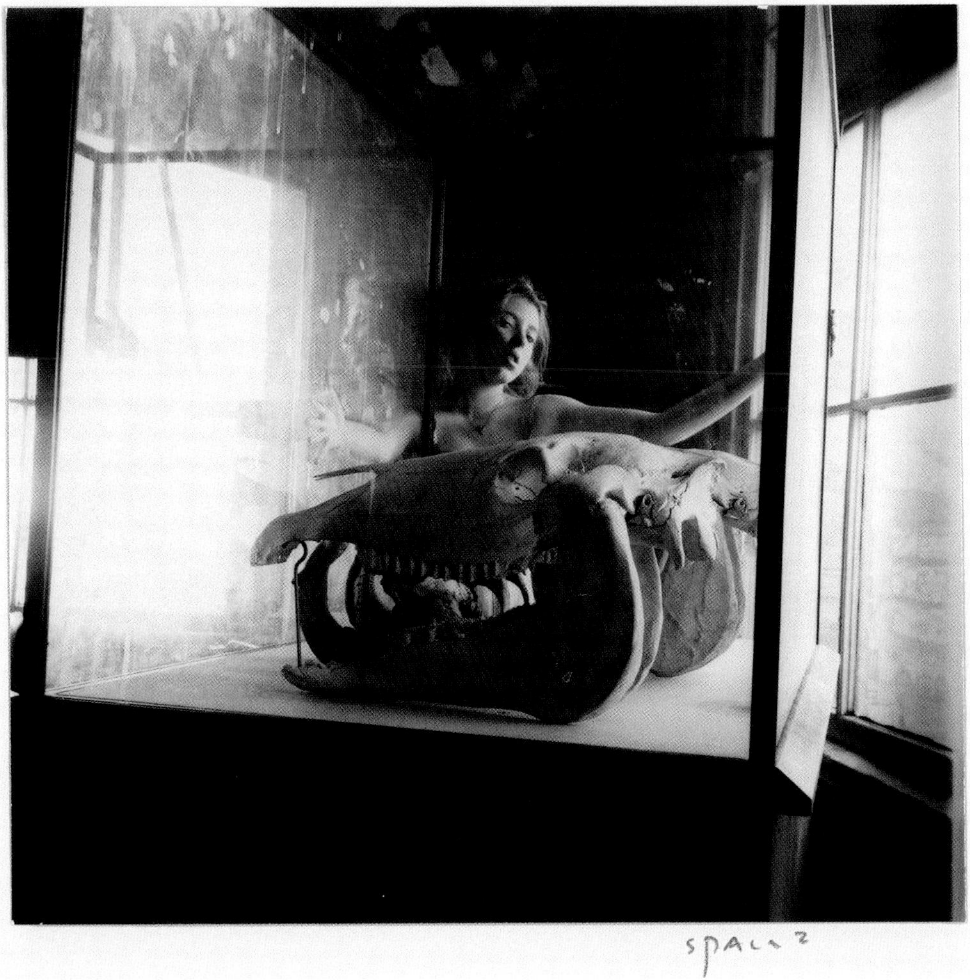

Space^2, Providence, Rhode Island, 1976

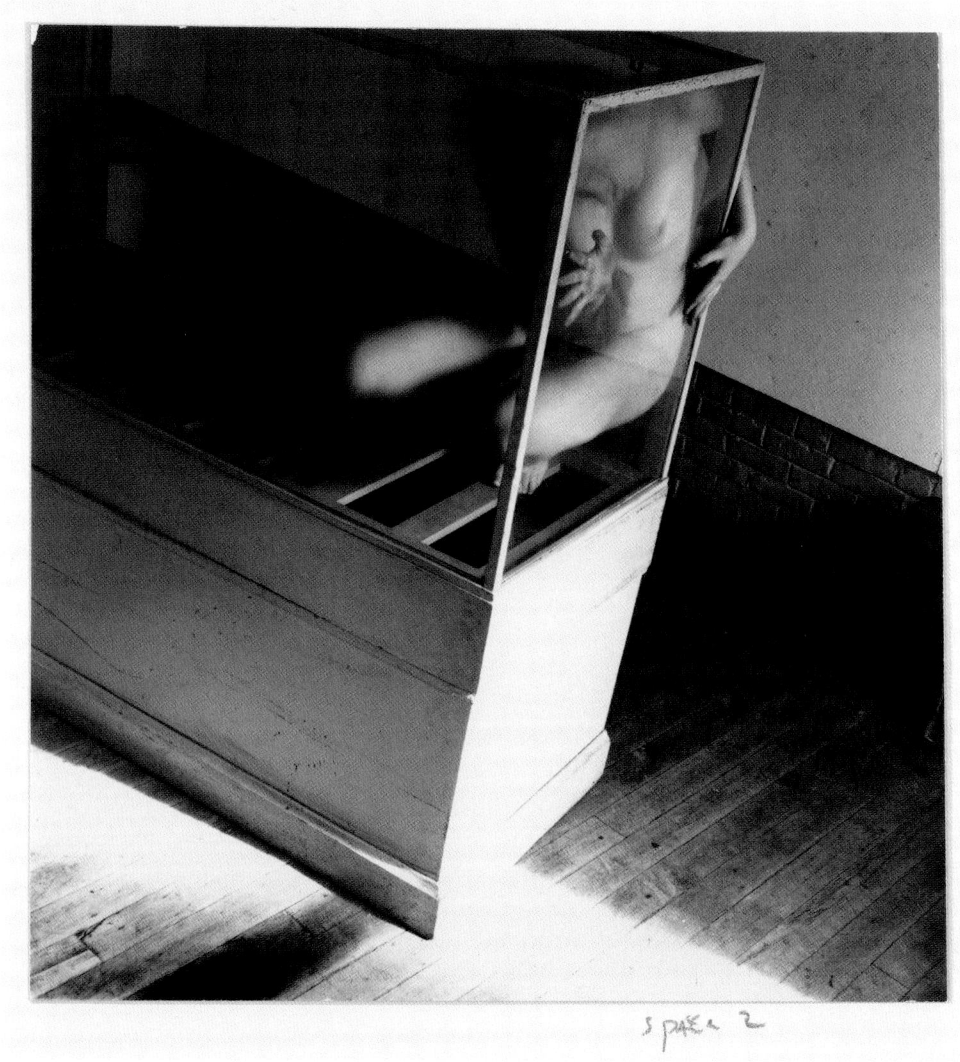

Space^2, Providence, Rhode Island, 1976

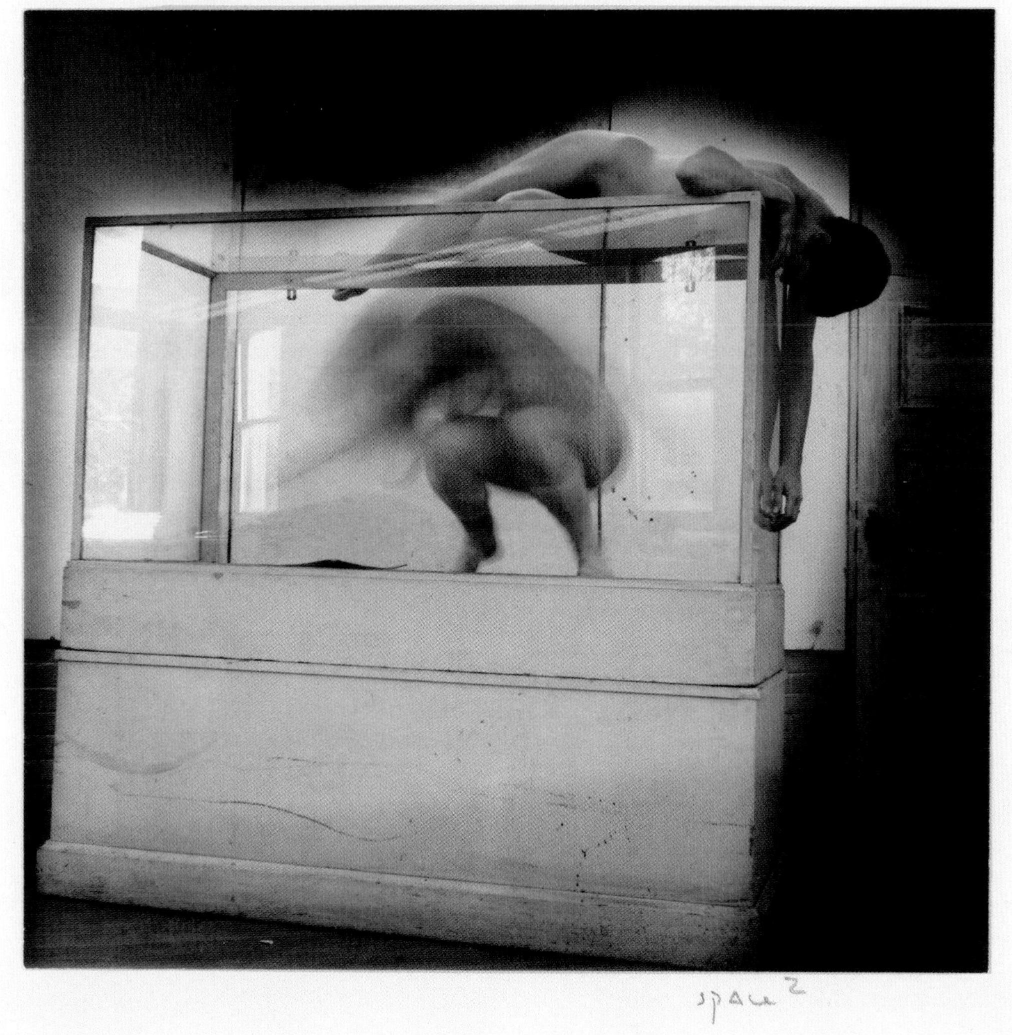

Space^2, Providence, Rhode Island, 1976

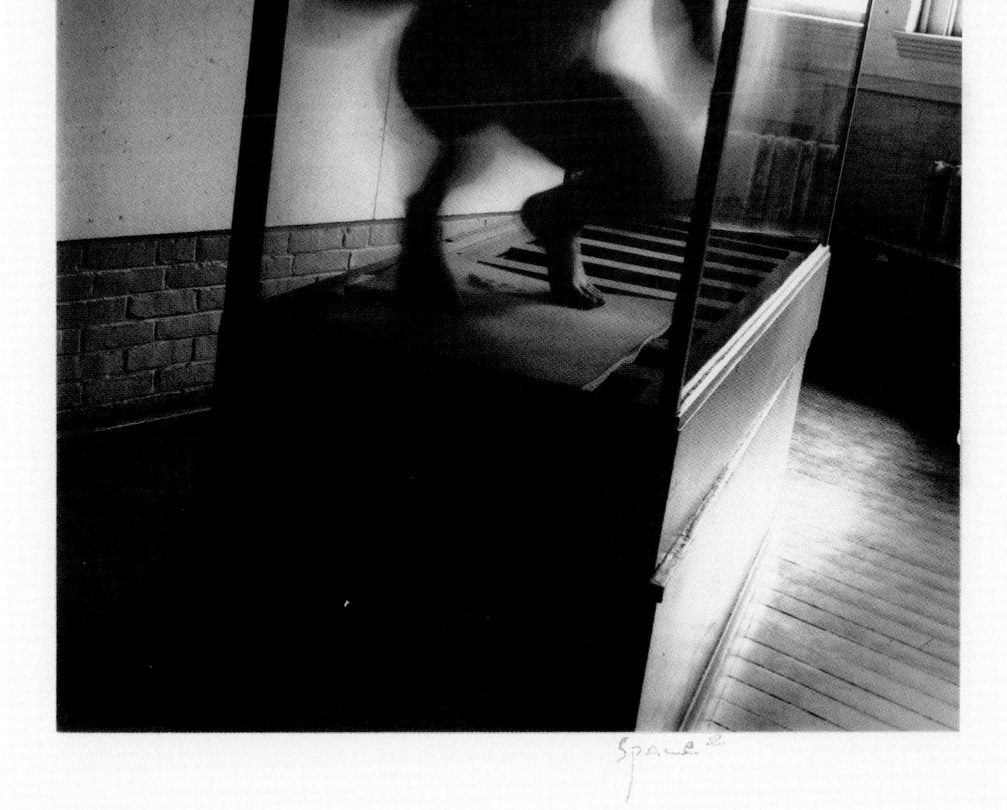

Space², Providence, Rhode Island, 1976

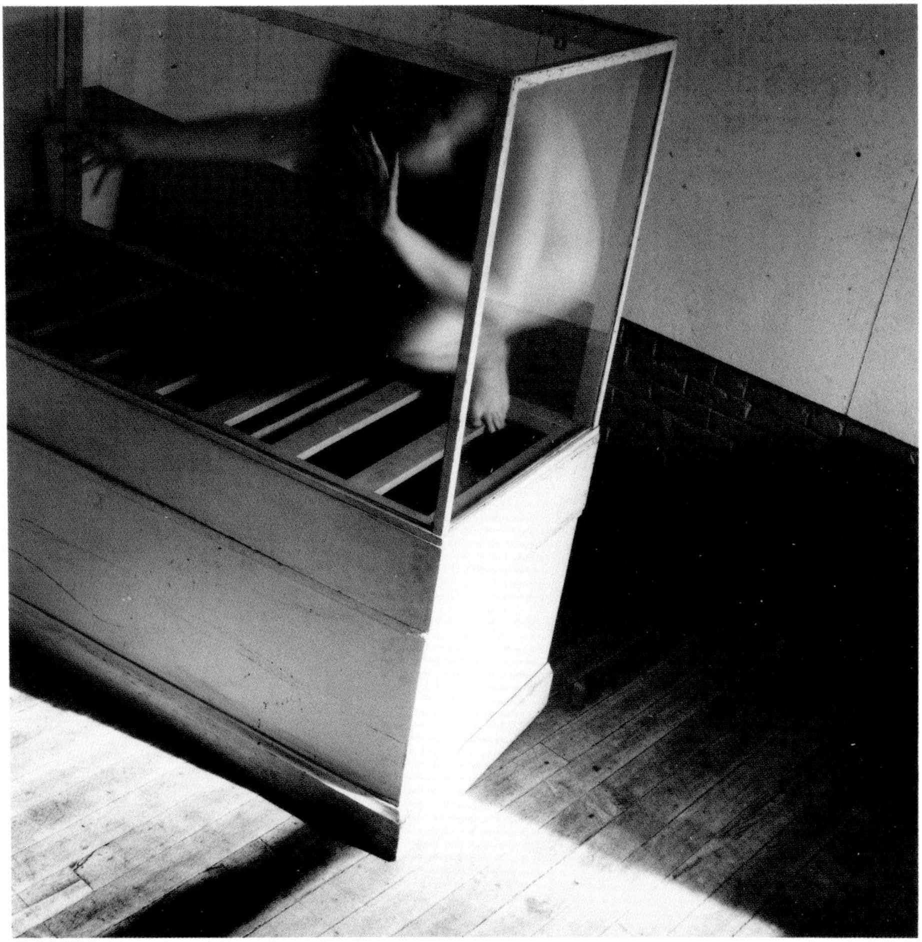

From Space[2], Providence, Rhode Island, 1976

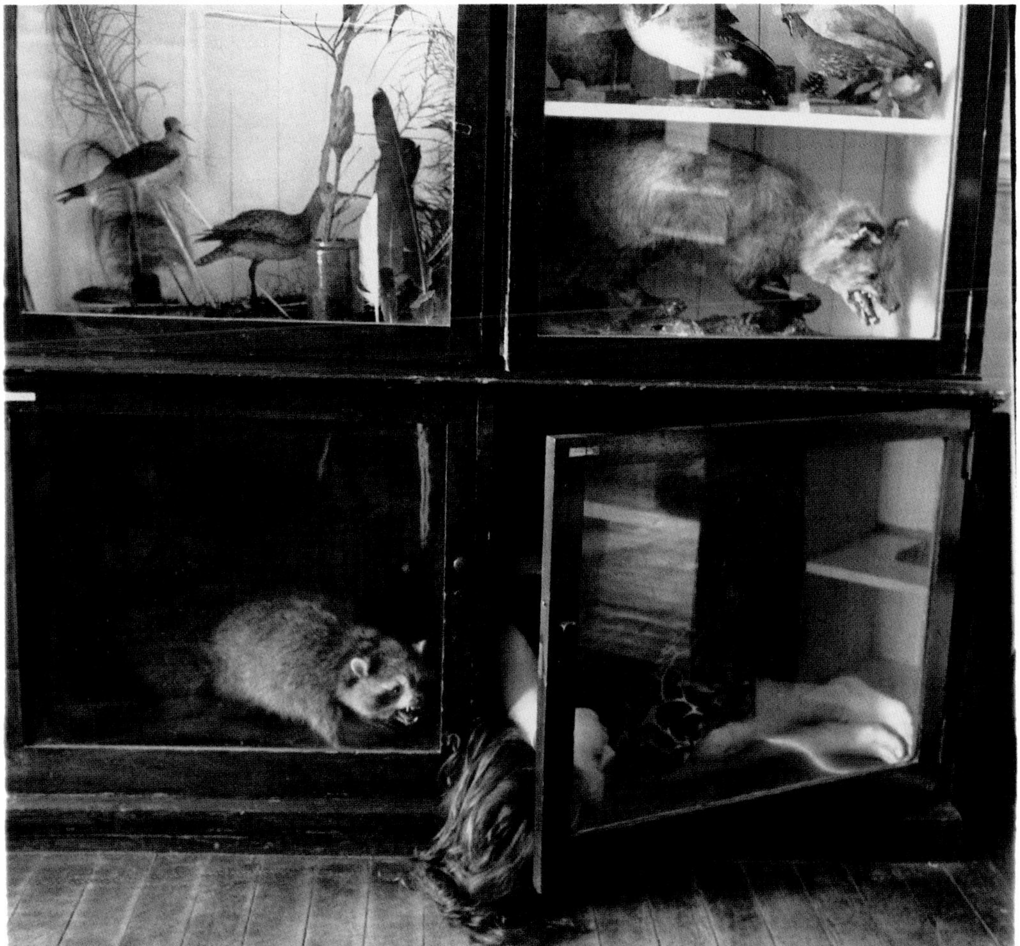

 Untitled, Providence, Rhode Island, 1975–78

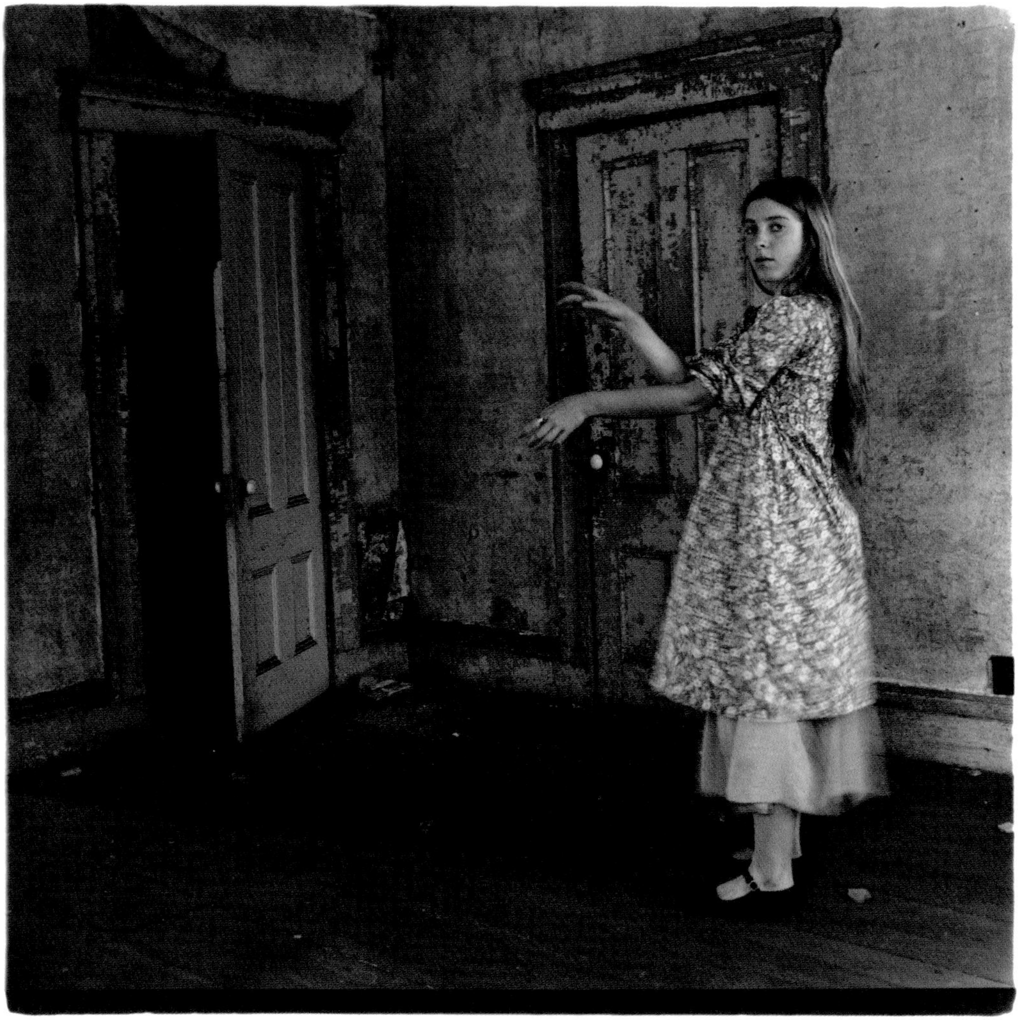

Untitled, Providence, Rhode Island, 1975–76

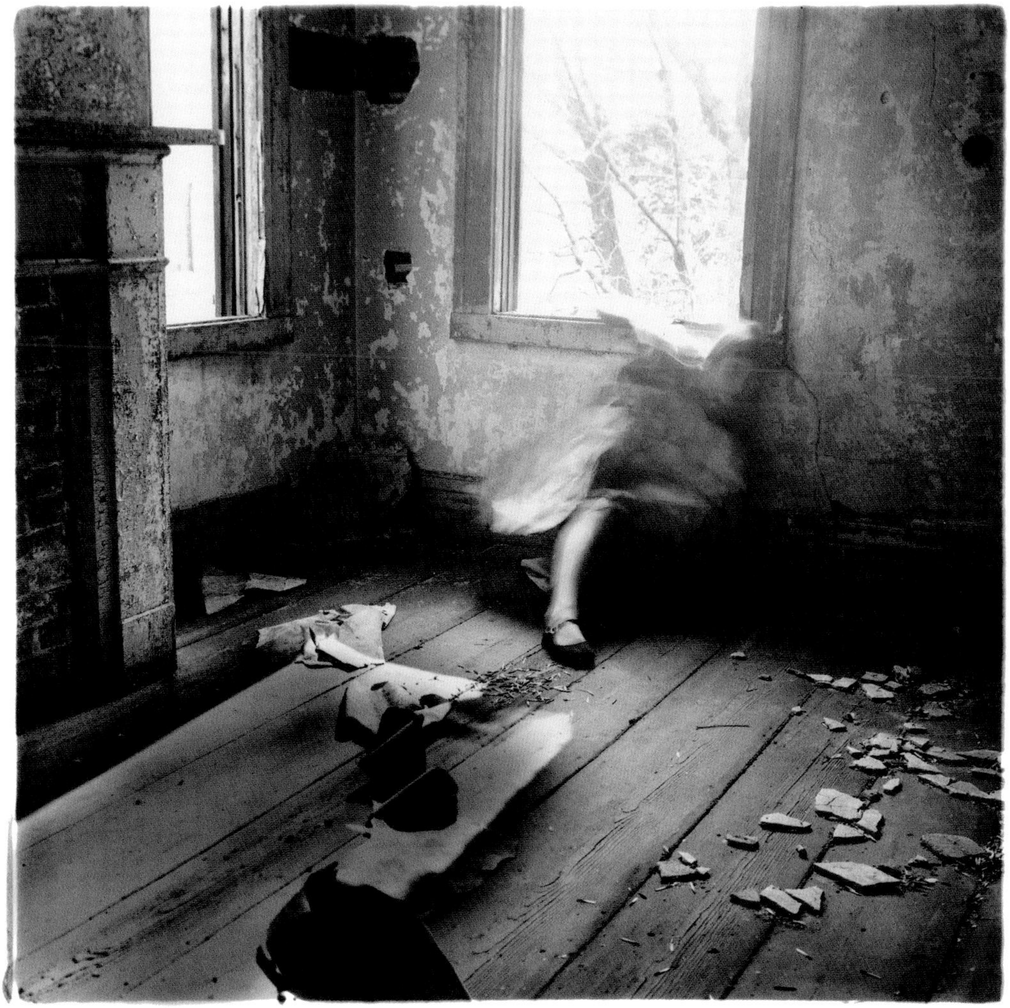

House #3, Providence, Rhode Island, 1976

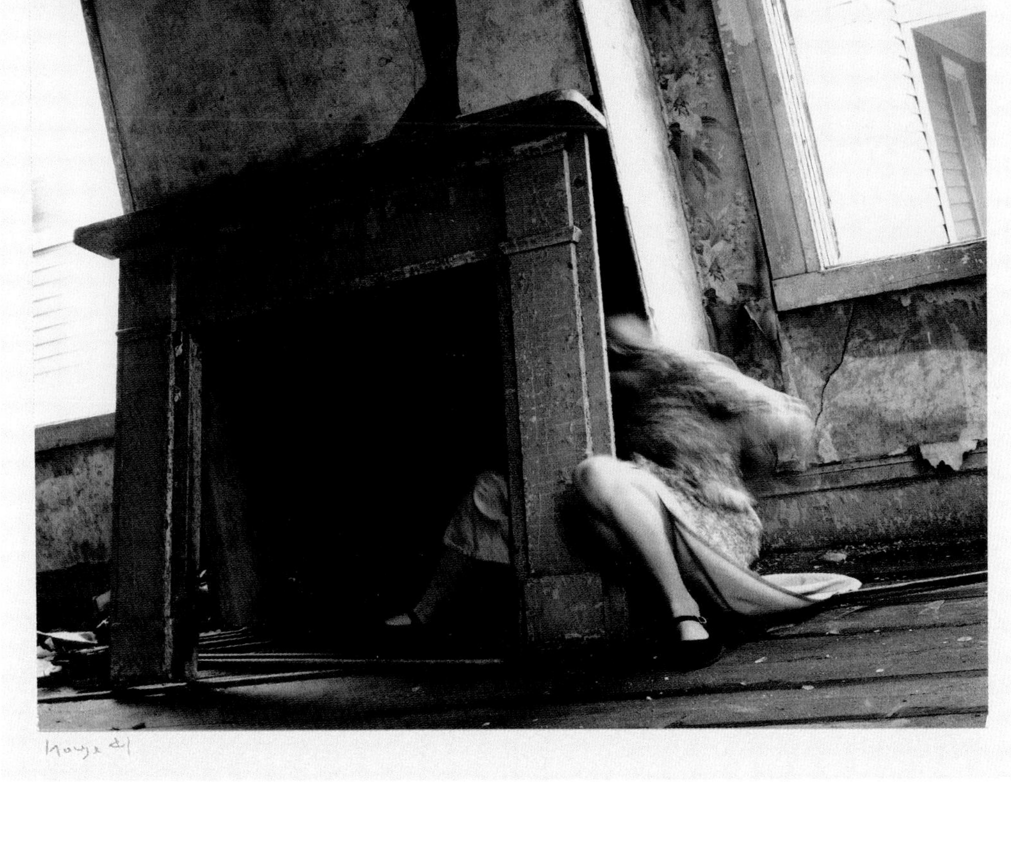

House #4, Providence, Rhode Island, 1976

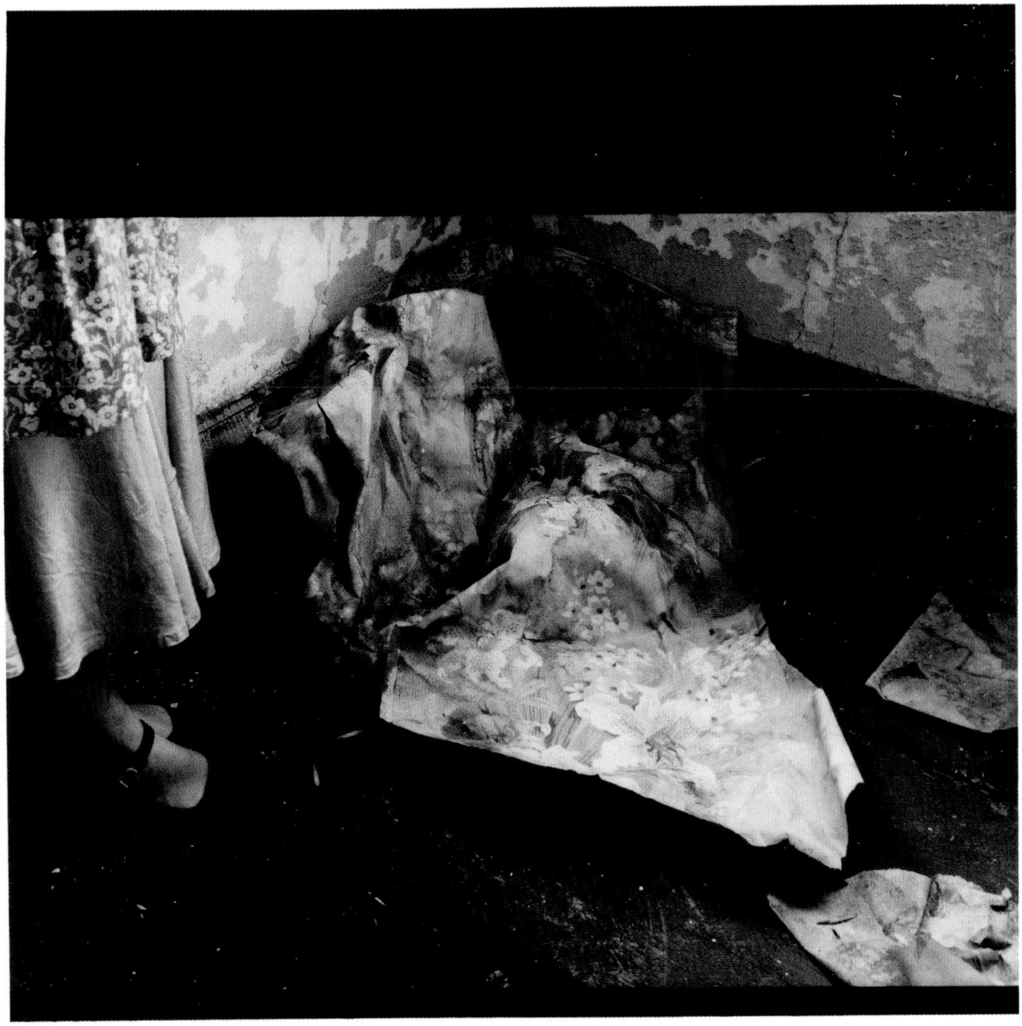

House #4, Providence, Rhode Island, 1976

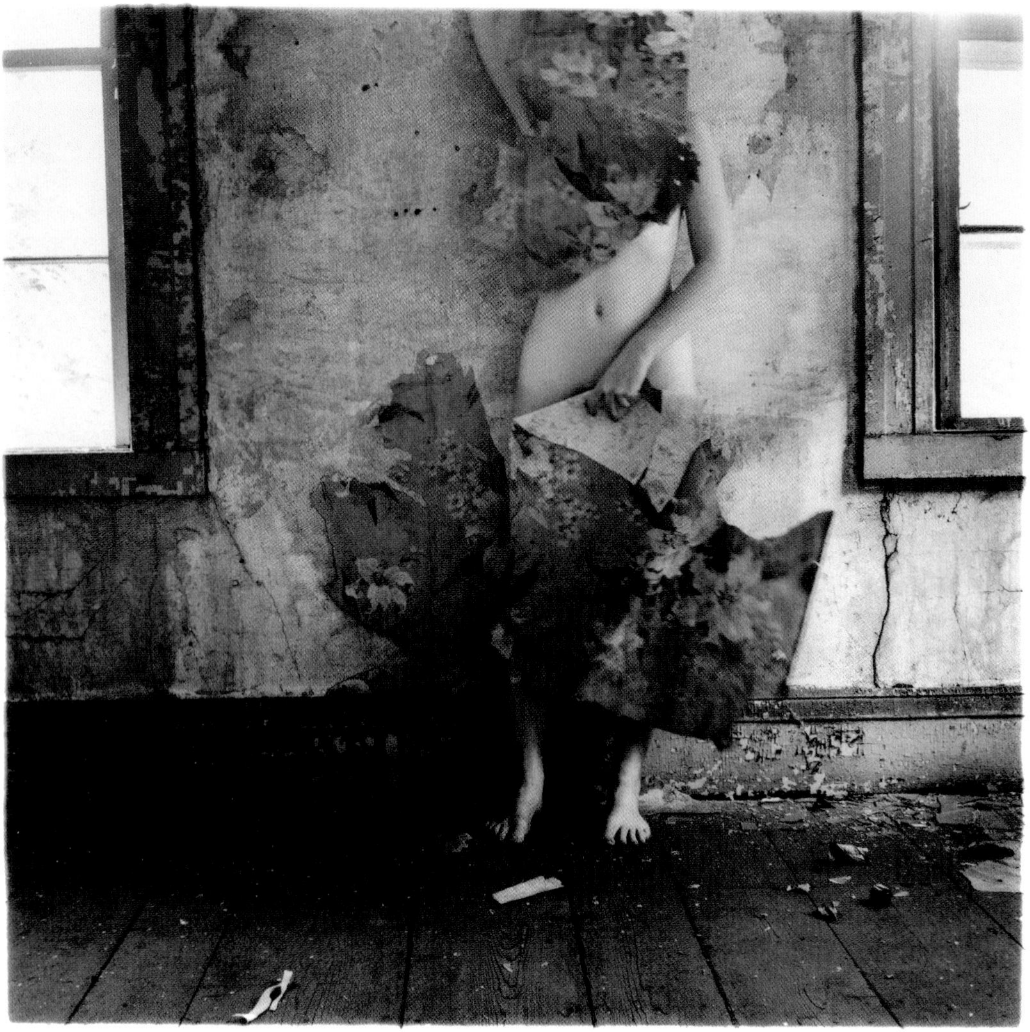

From Space², Providence, Rhode Island, 1976

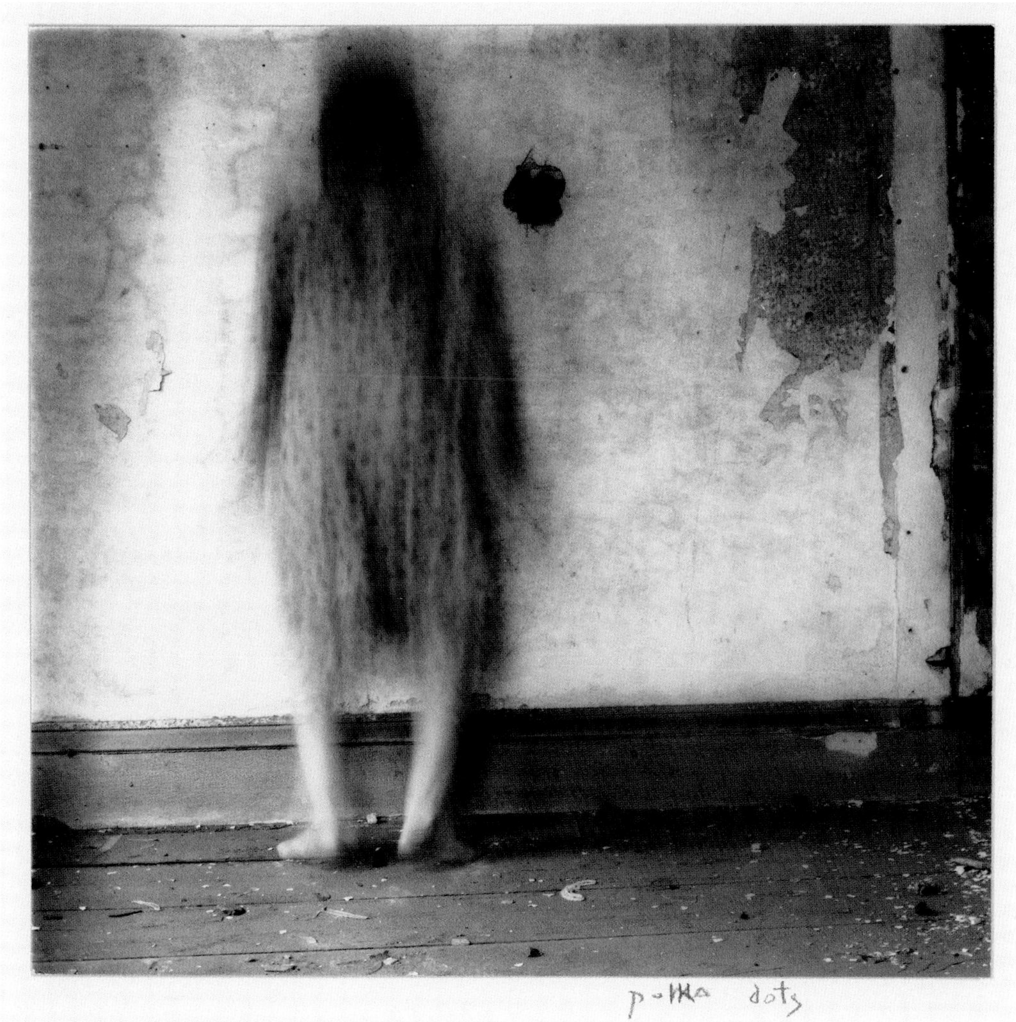

Polka Dots, Providence, Rhode Island, 1976

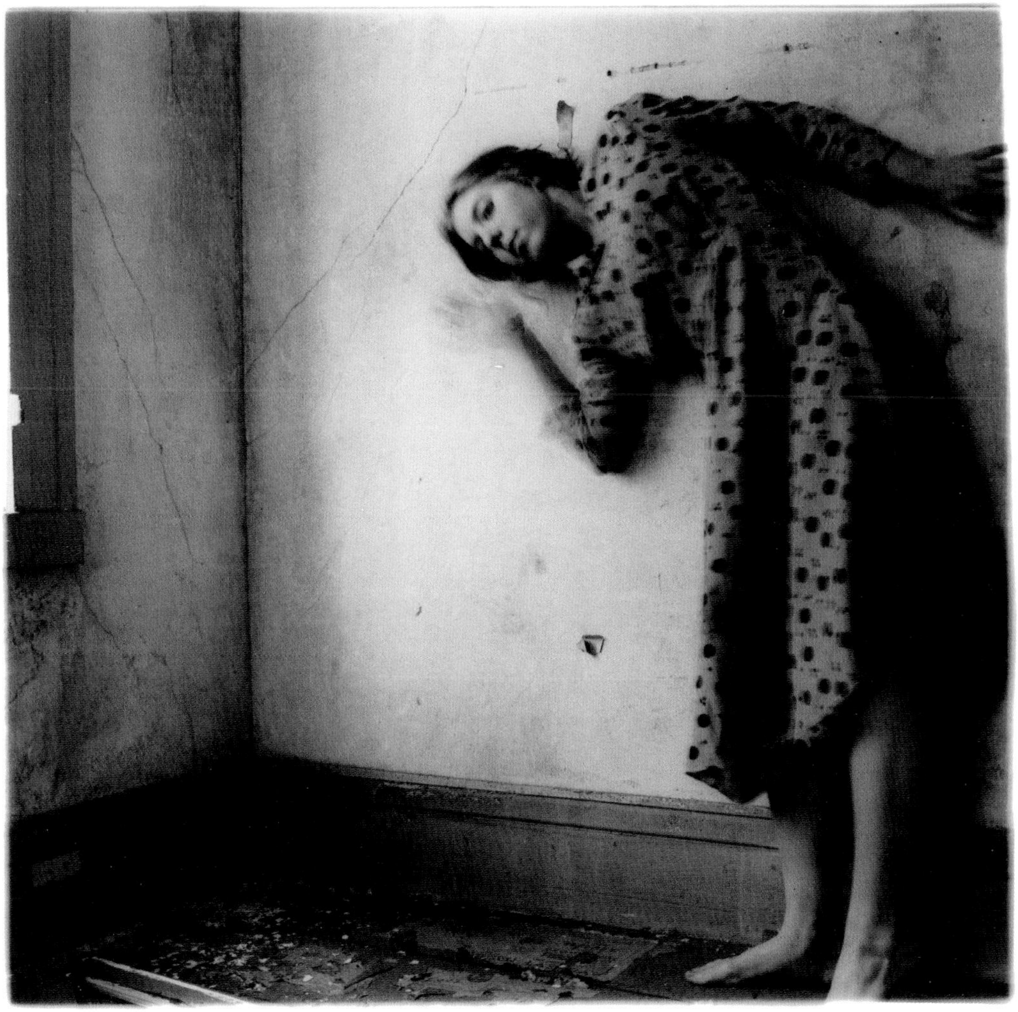

Polka Dots #5, Providence, Rhode Island, 1976

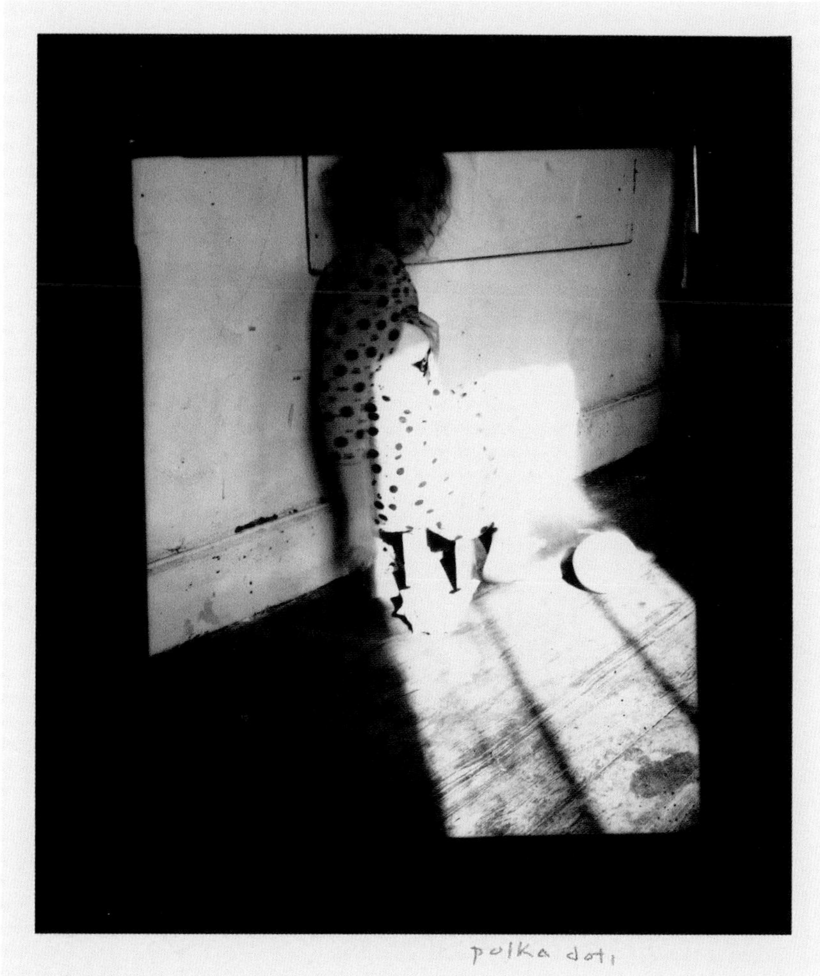

Polka Dots, Providence, Rhode Island, 1976

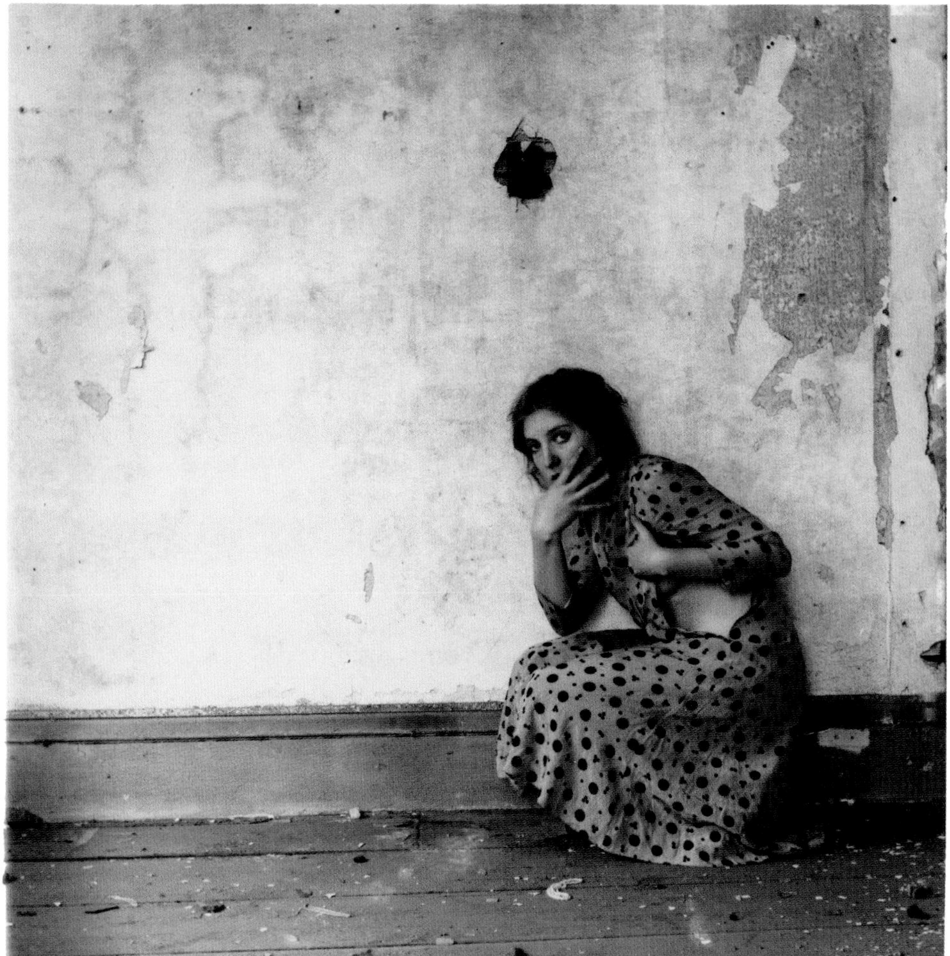

 From Polka Dots, Providence, Rhode Island, 1976

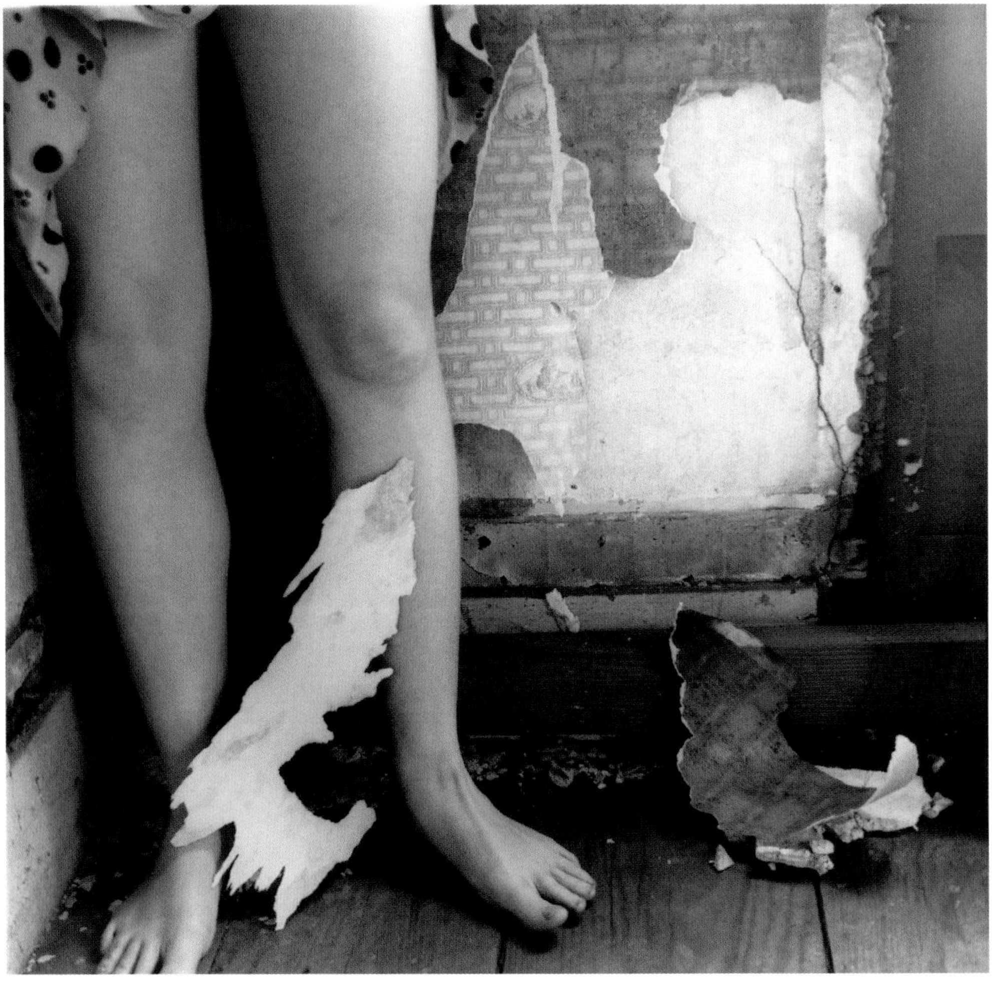

Lightning Legs, Providence, Rhode Island, 1976

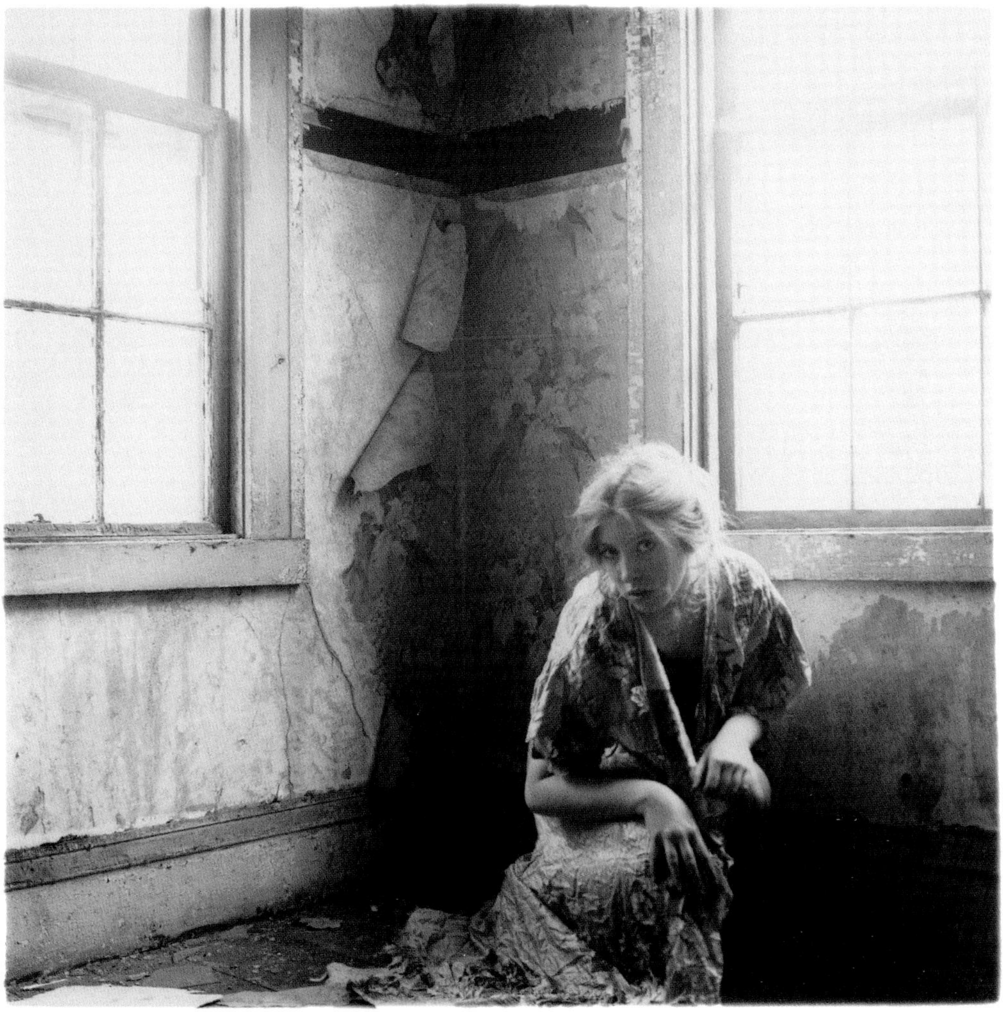

 Untitled, Providence, Rhode Island, 1975–78

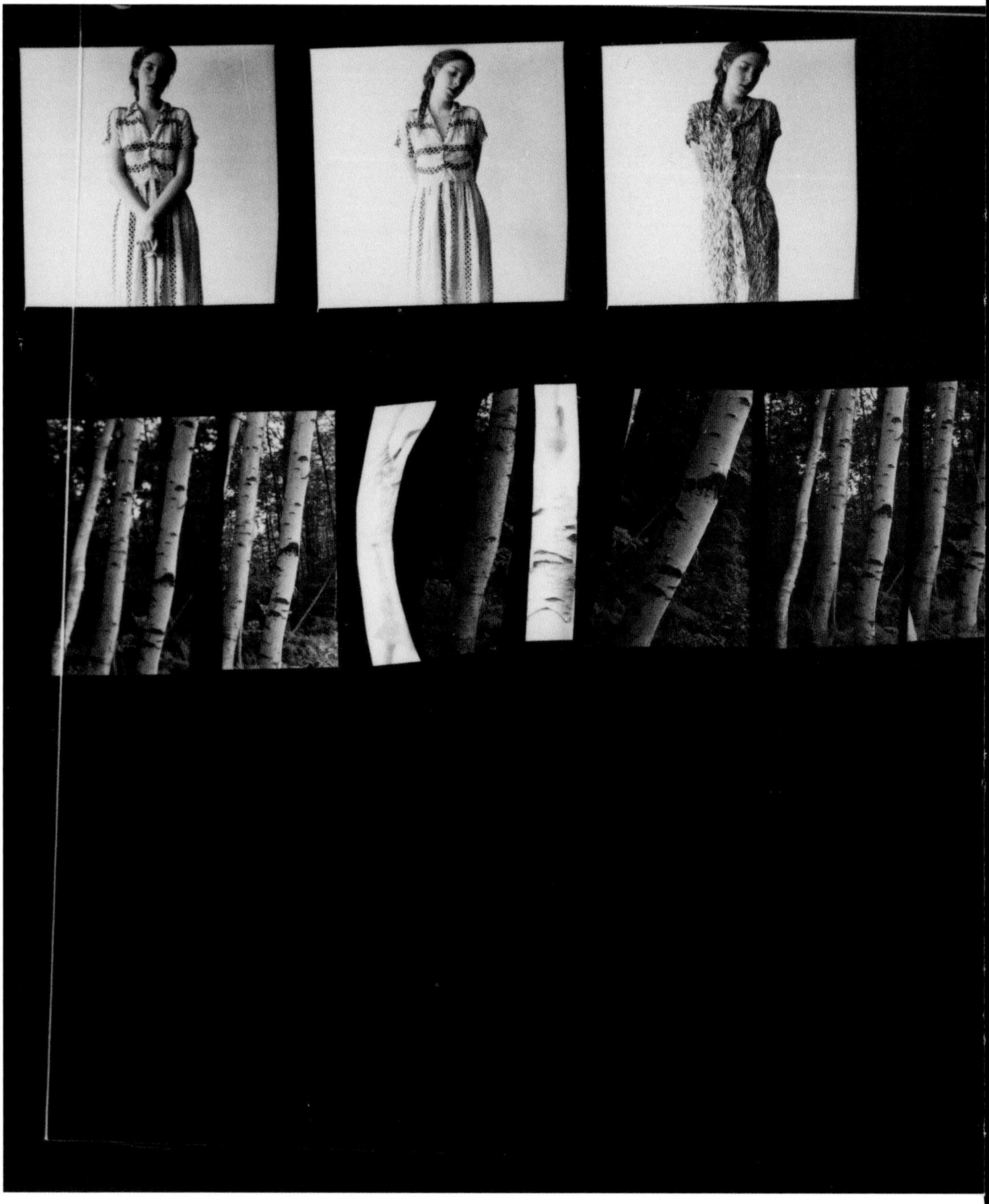

Untitled, MacDowell Colony, Peterborough, New Hampshire, 1980

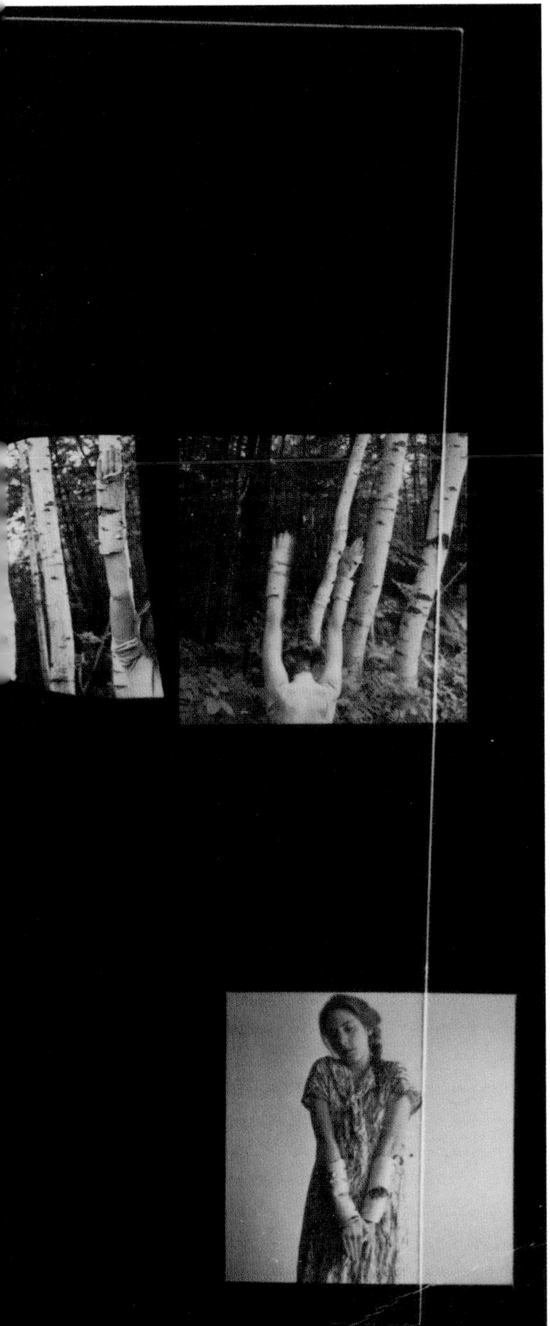

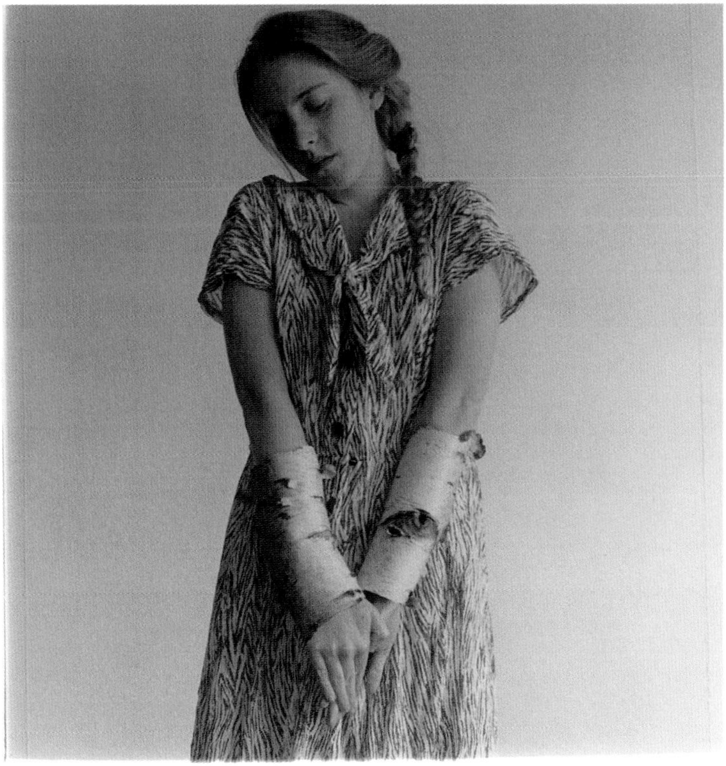

Untitled, MacDowell Colony, Peterborough, New Hampshire, 1980

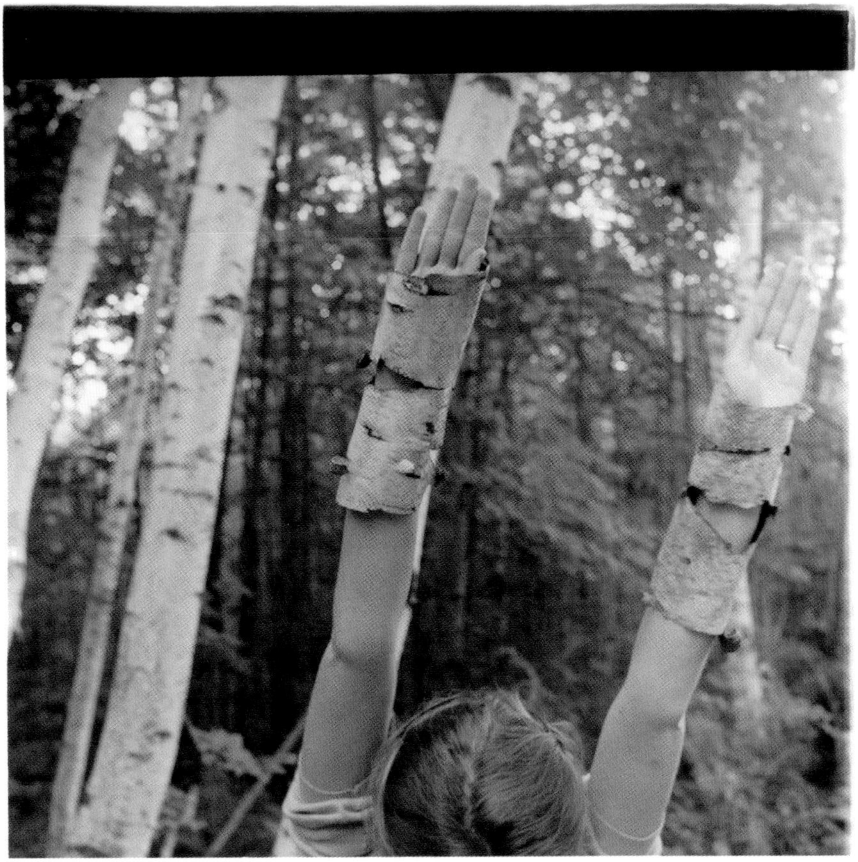

 Untitled, MacDowell Colony, Peterborough, New Hampshire, 1980

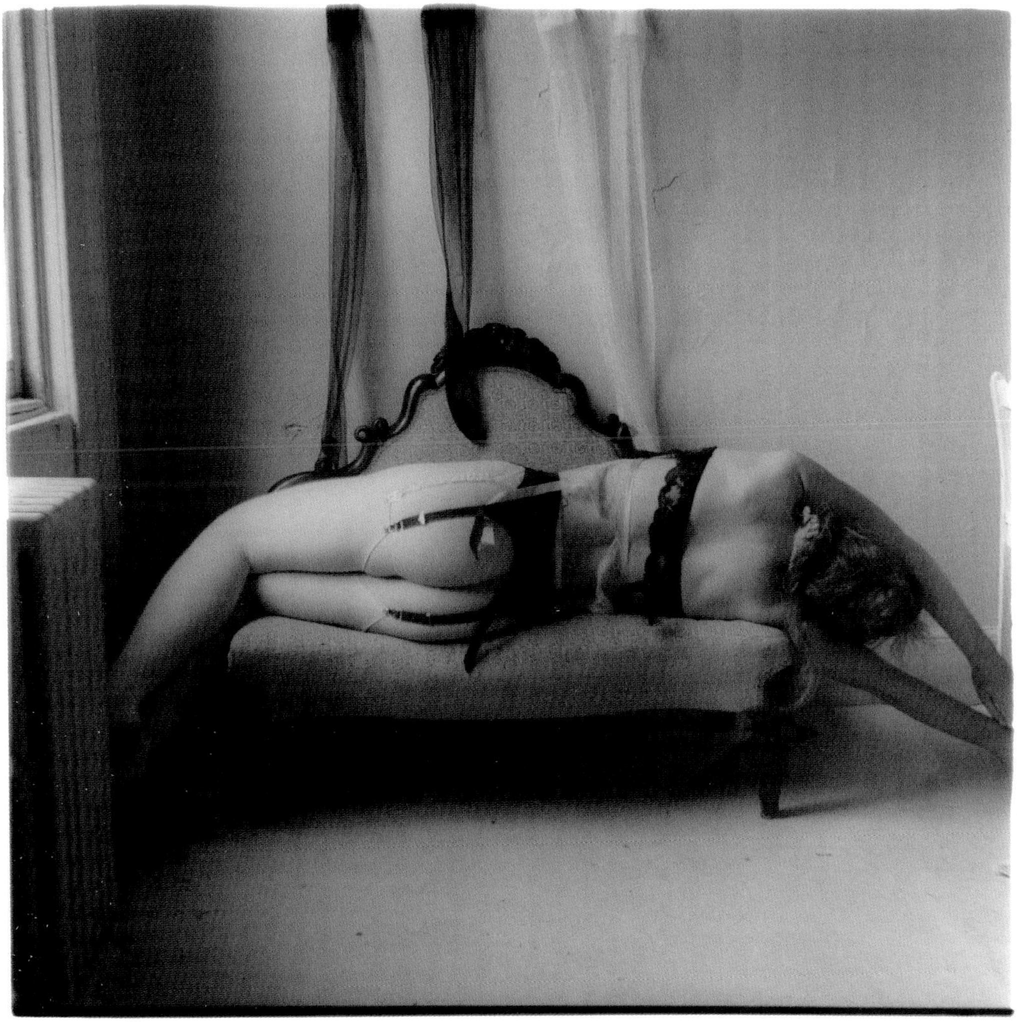

Untitled, New York, 1979–80

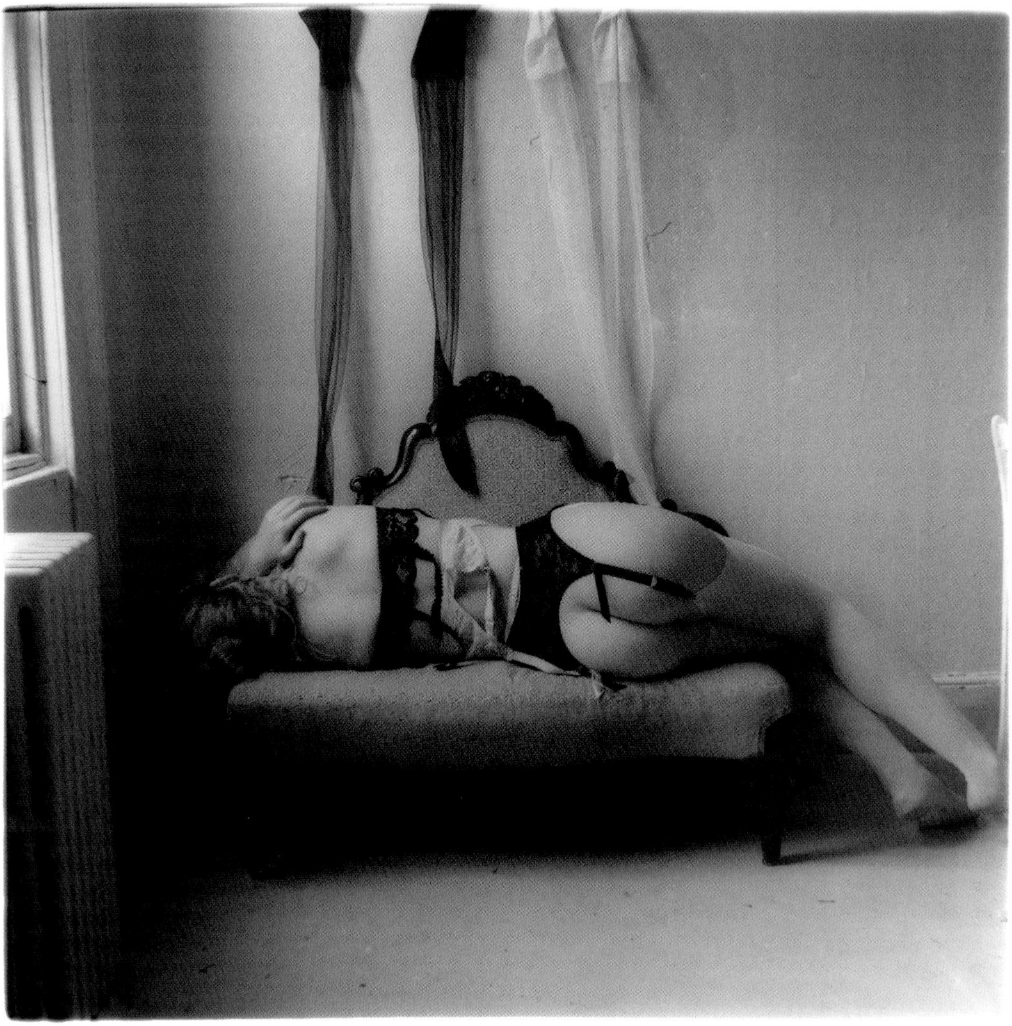

Untitled, New York, 1979–80

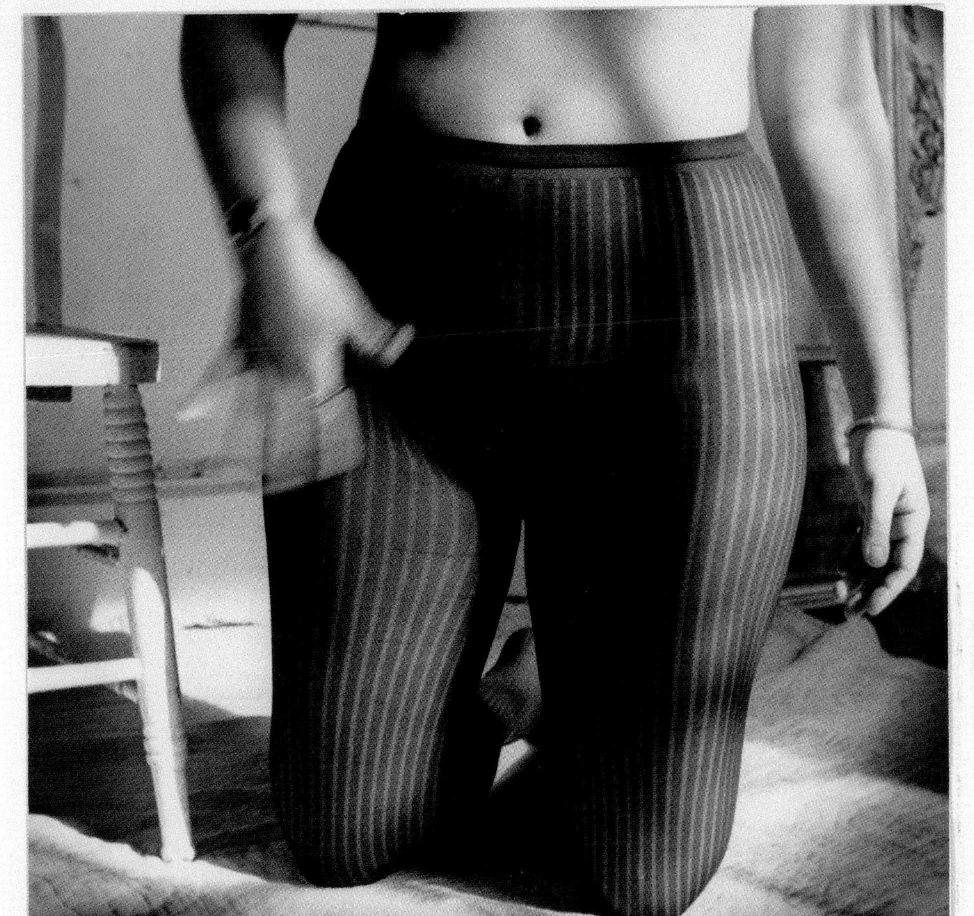

Verticale, Providence, Rhode Island, 1976

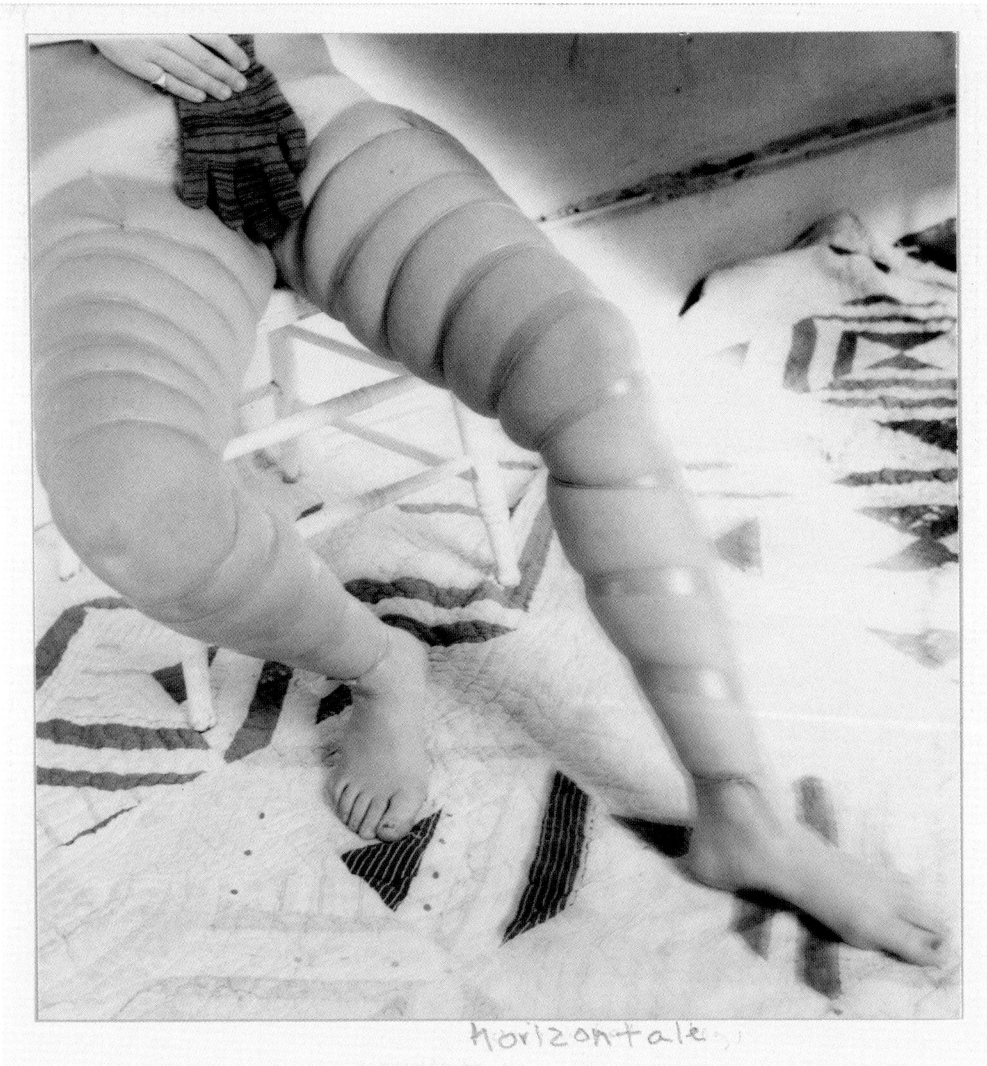

Horizontale, Providence, Rhode Island, 1976

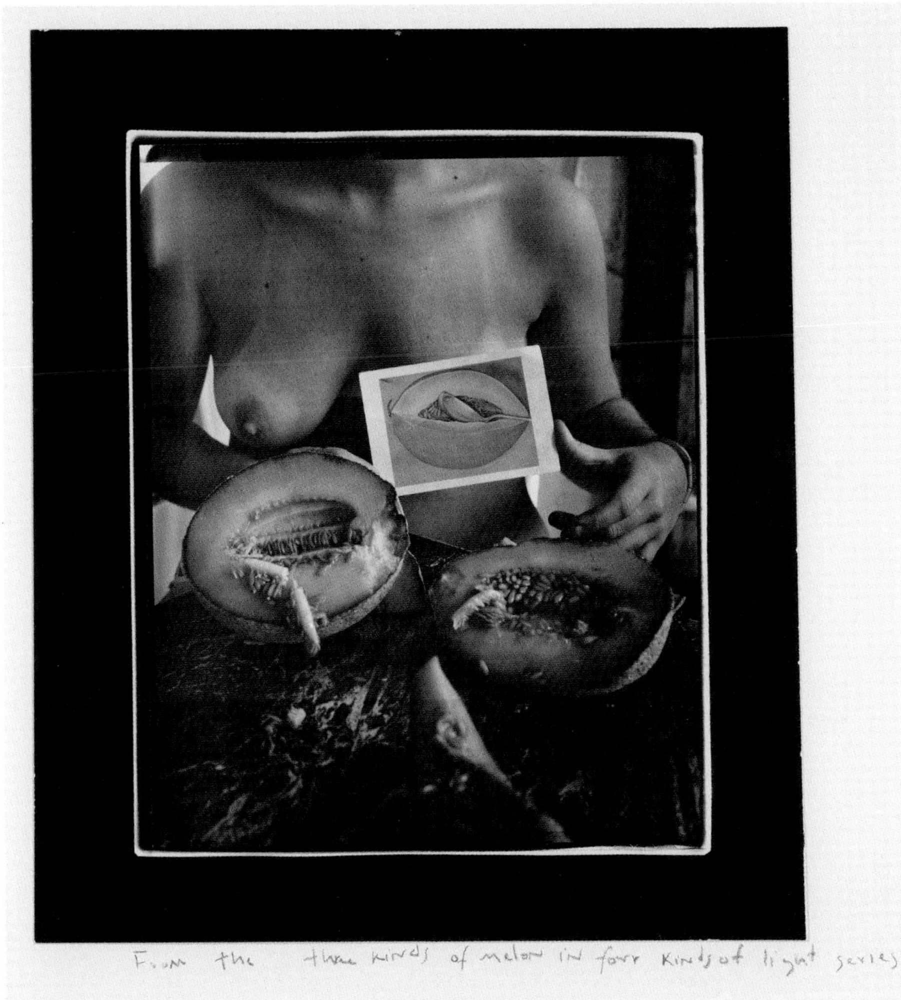

From the three kinds of melon in four kinds of light series, Providence, Rhode Island, 1976

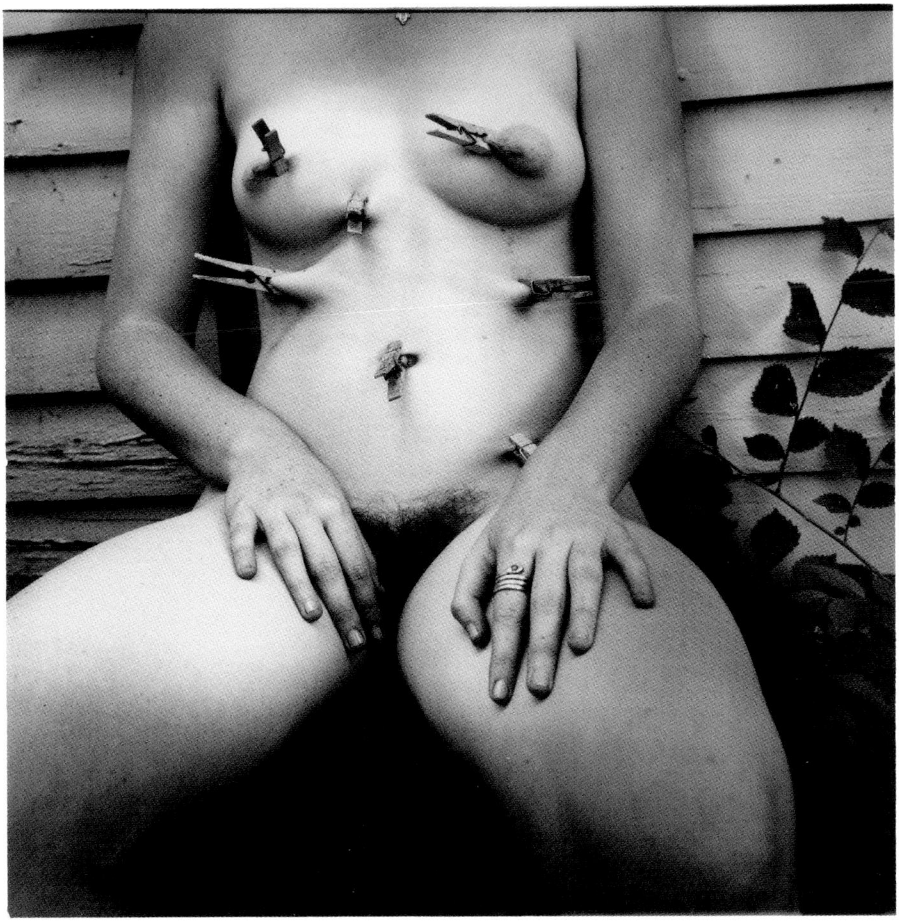

Untitled, Boulder, Colorado, 1976

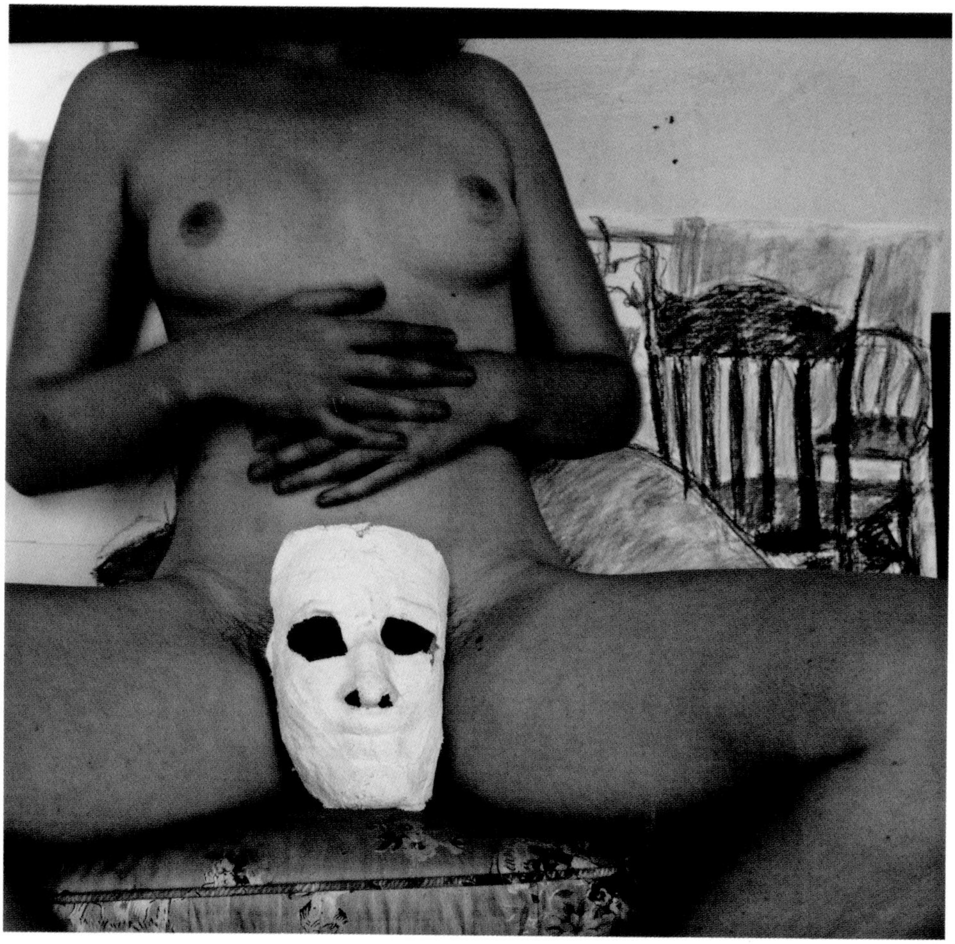

Face, Providence, Rhode Island, 1976

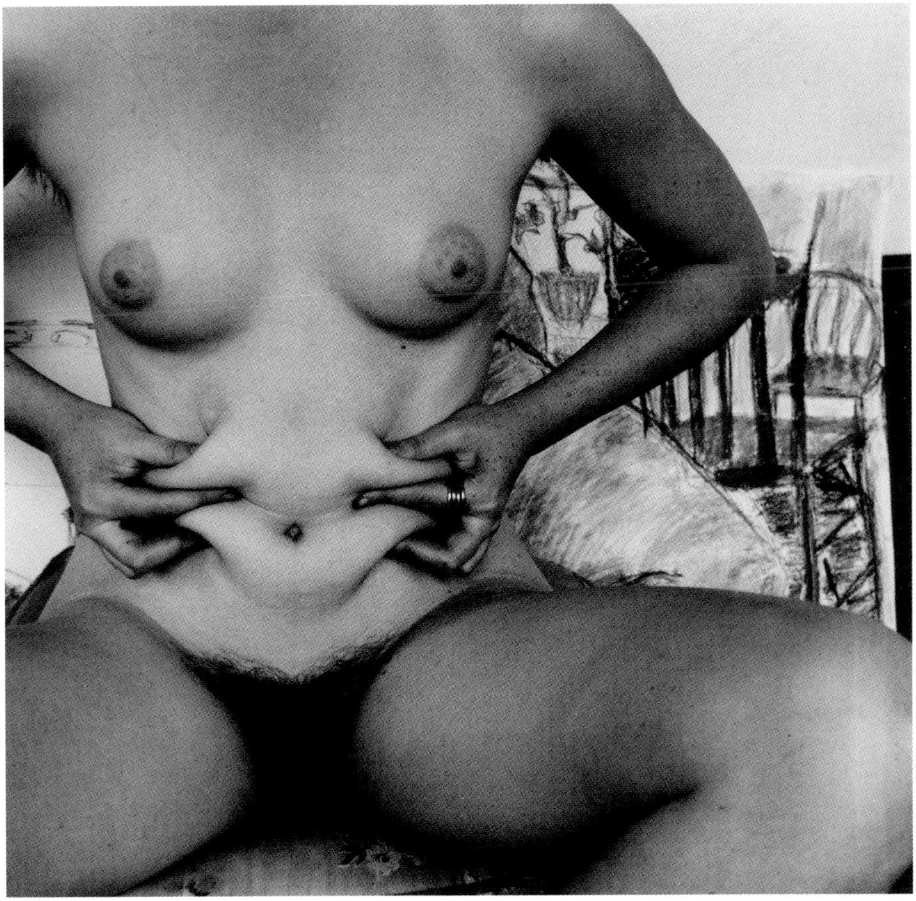

Untitled, Providence, Rhode Island, 1976

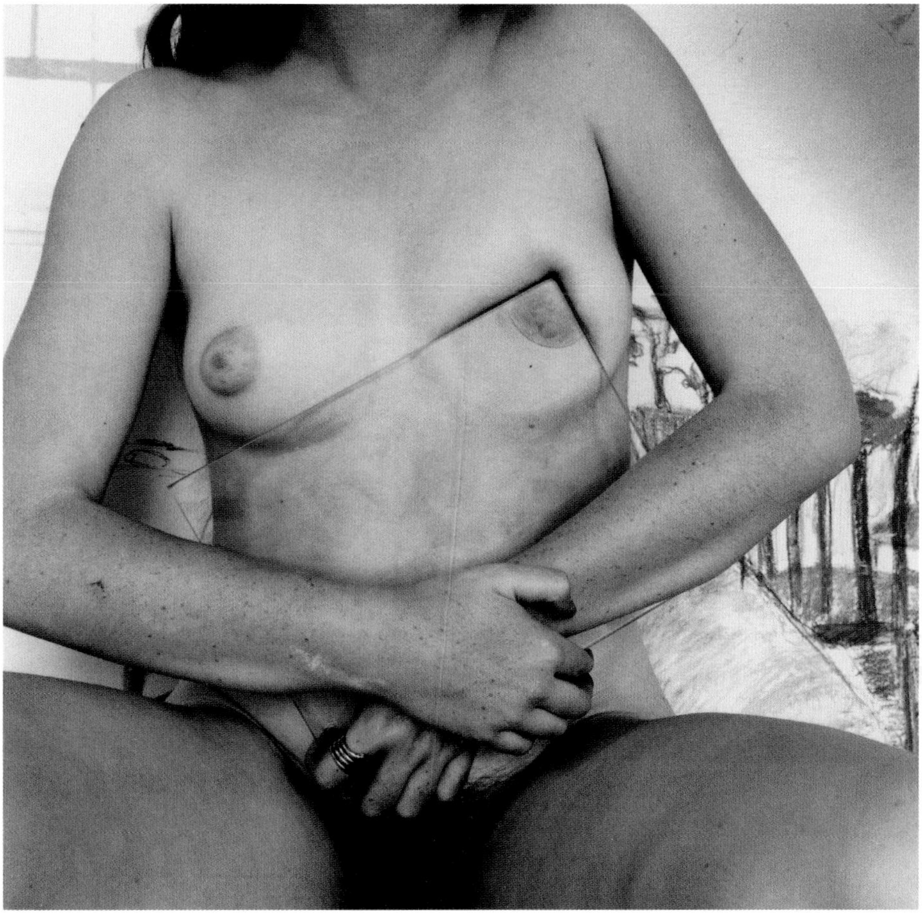

 Untitled, Providence, Rhode Island, 1976

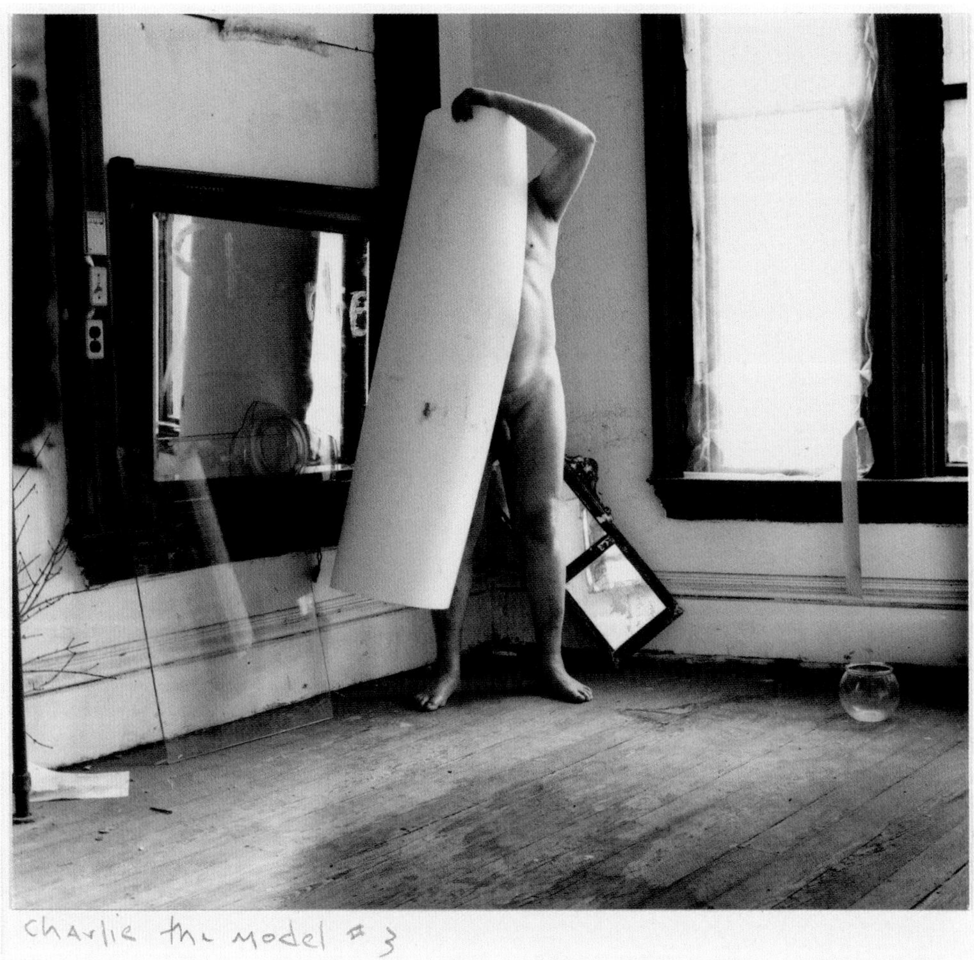

Charlie the Model #3, Providence, Rhode Island, 1976–77

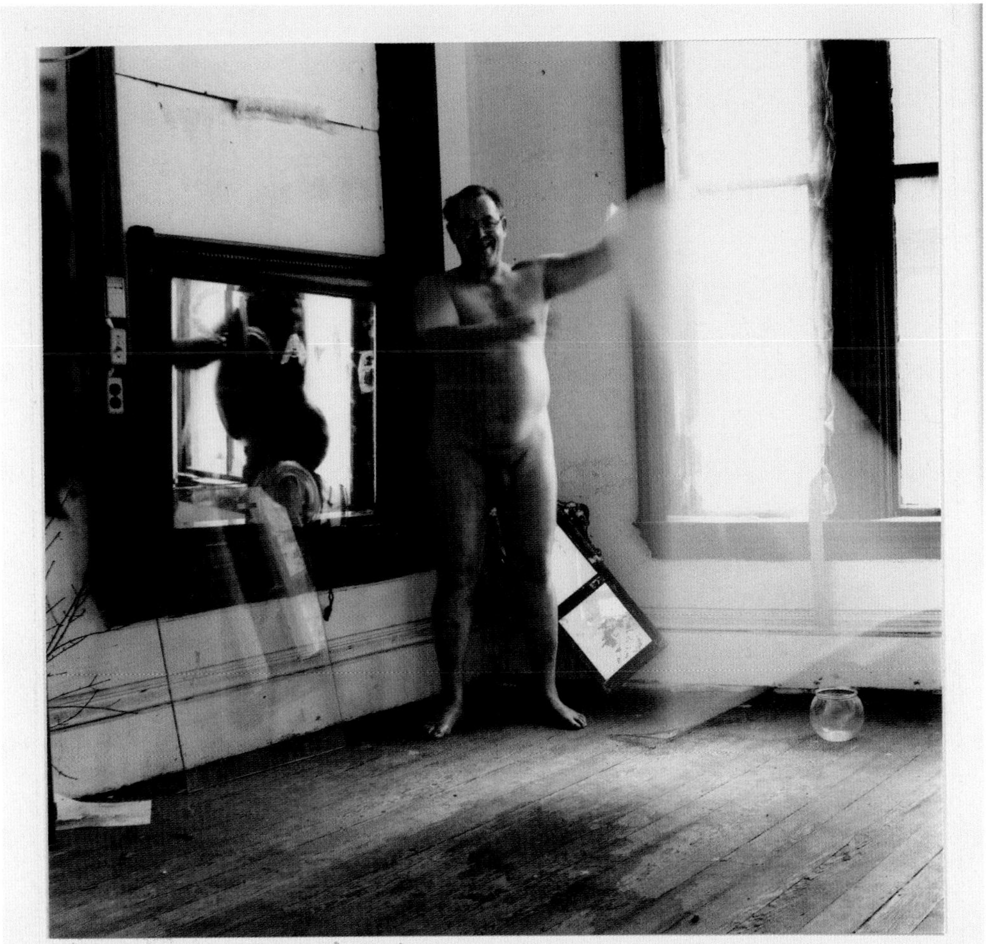

Charlie the Model #4, Providence, Rhode Island, 1976–77

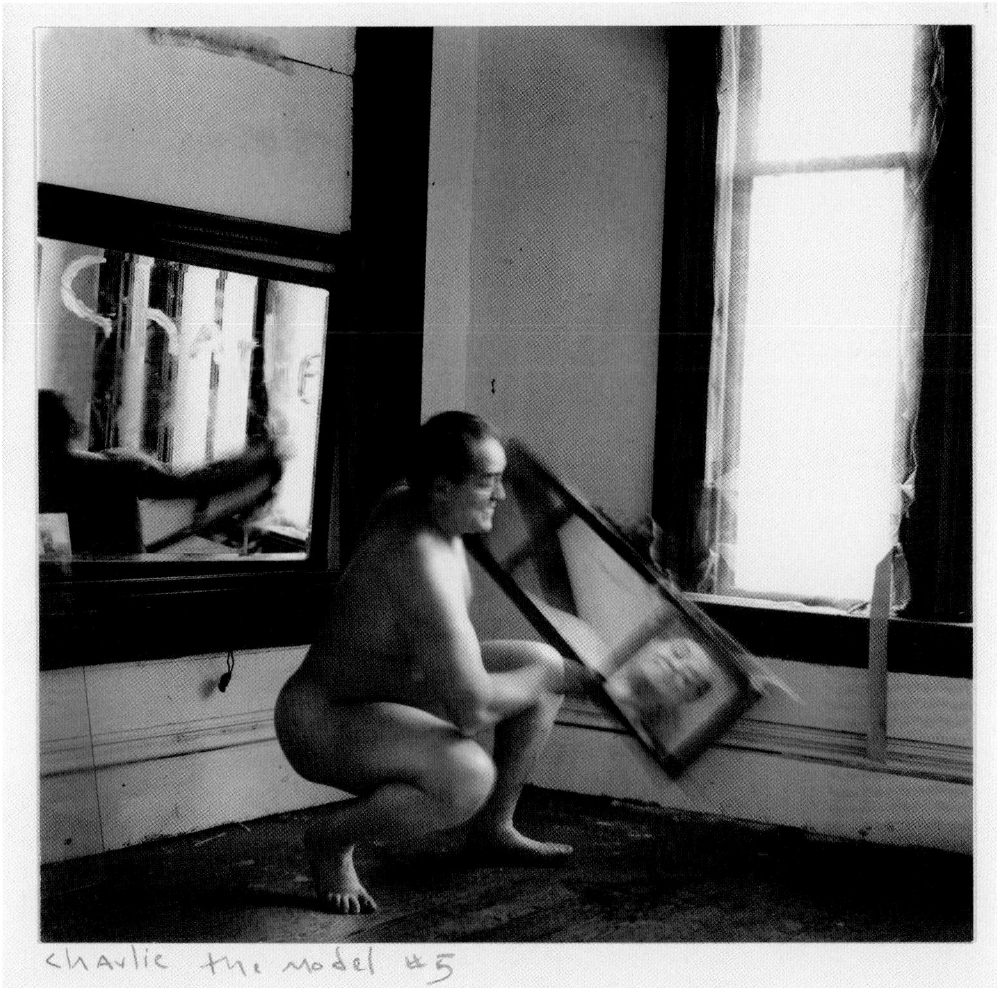

 Charlie the Model #5, Providence, Rhode Island, 1976–77

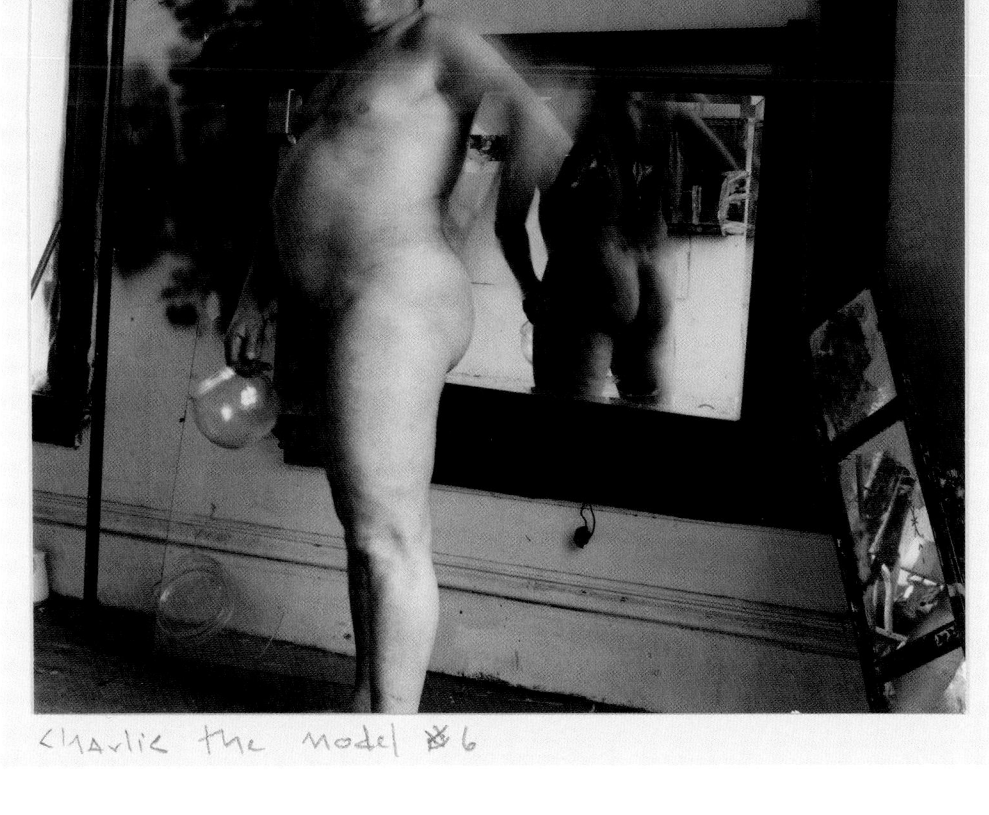

Charlie the Model #6, Providence, Rhode Island, 1976–77

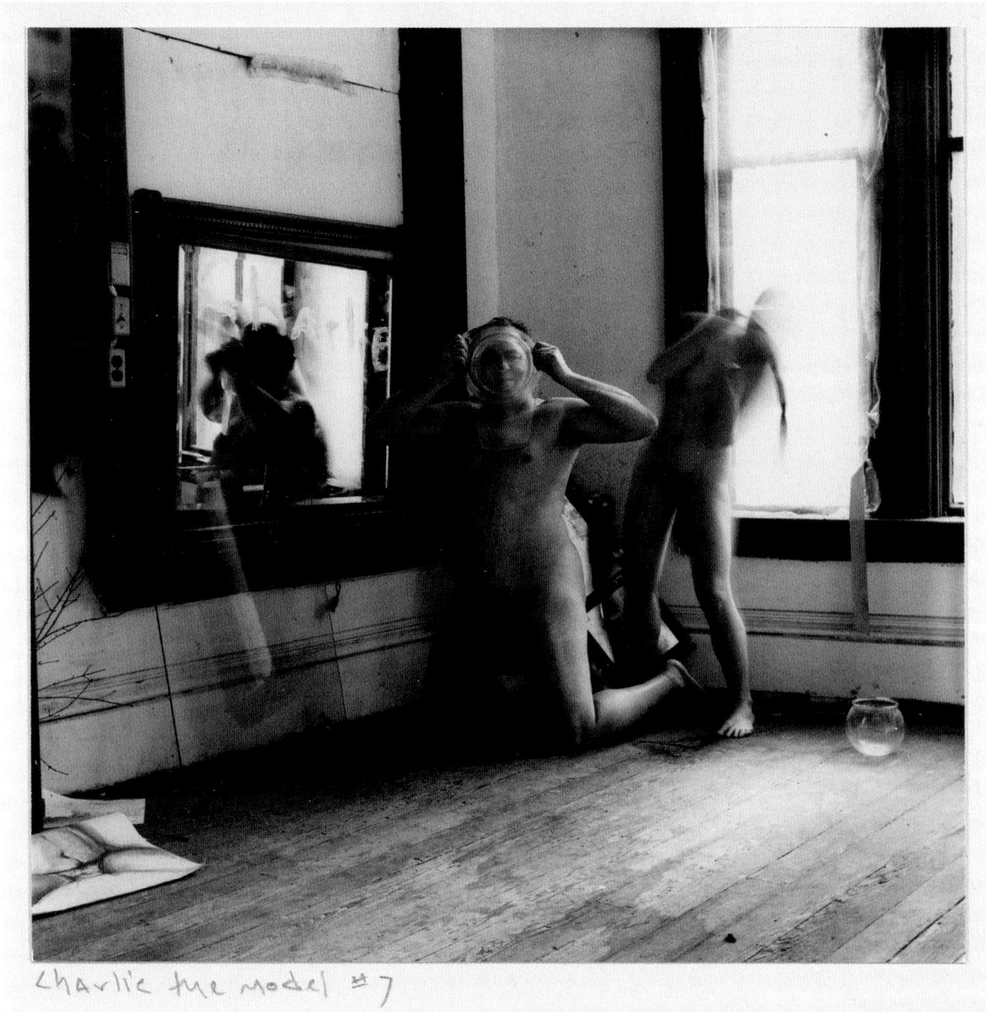

Charlie the Model #7, Providence, Rhode Island, 1976–77

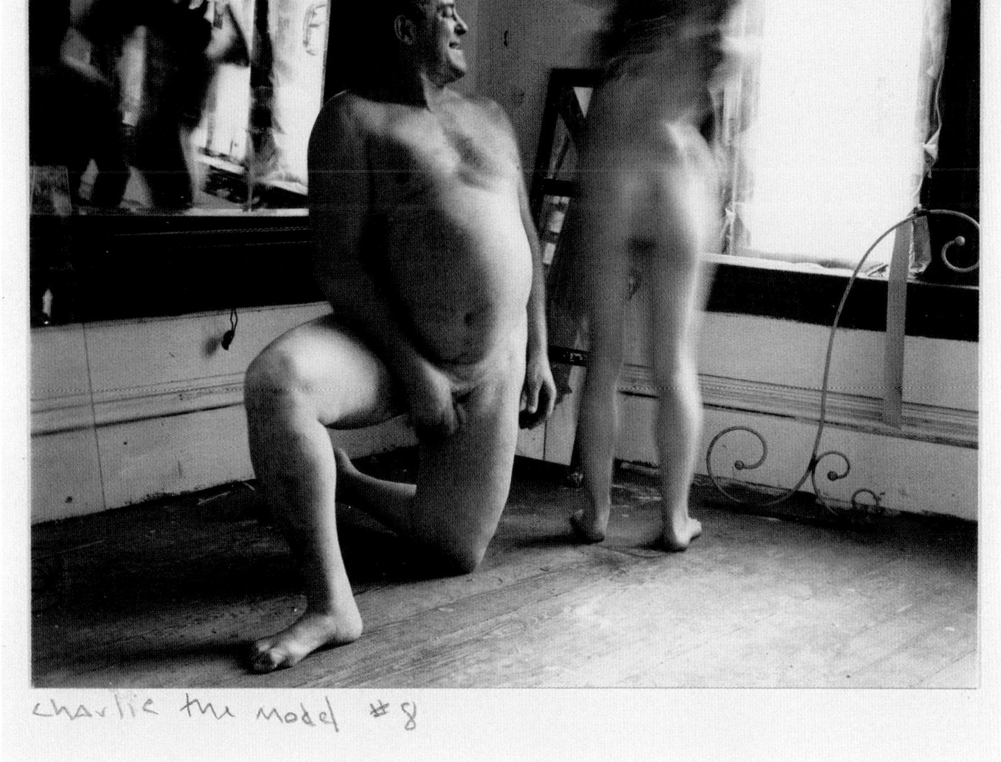

 Charlie the Model #8, Providence, Rhode Island, 1976–77

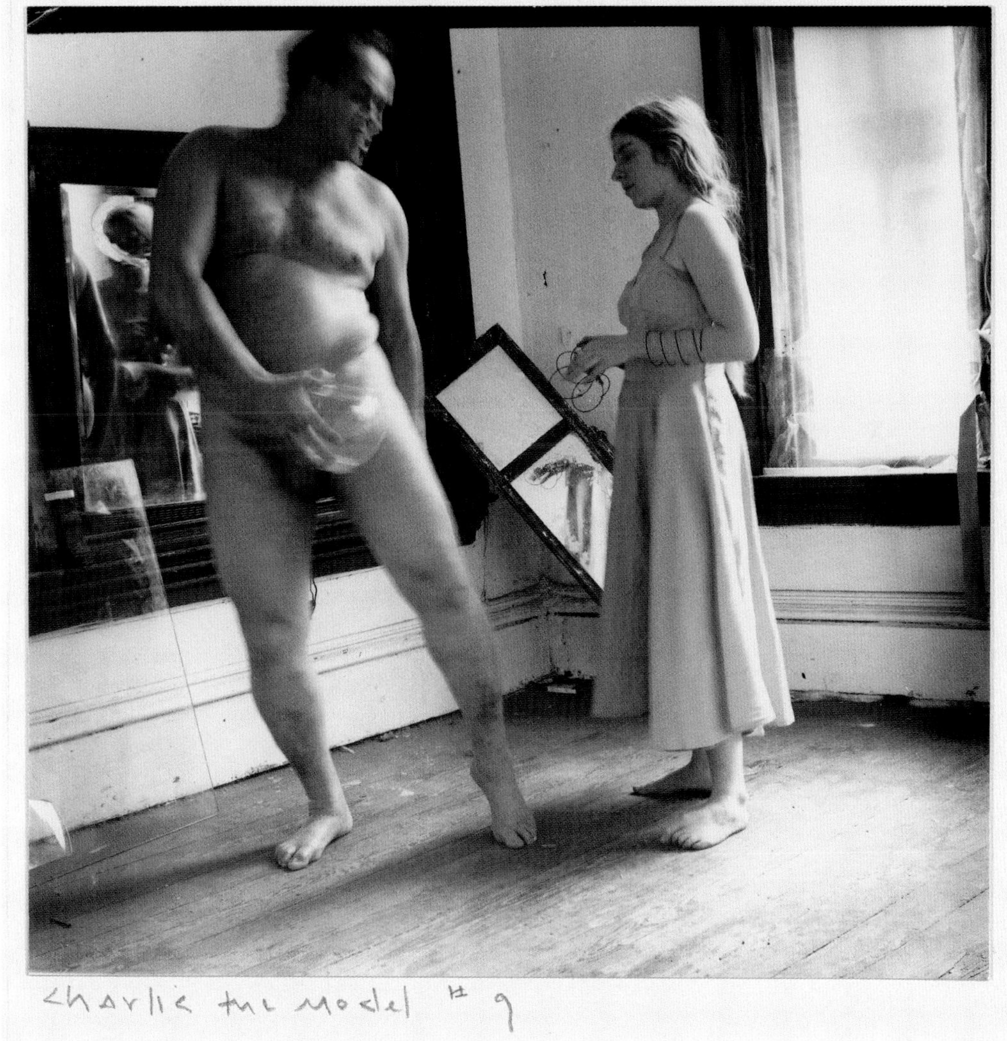

Charlie the Model #9, Providence, Rhode Island, 1976–77

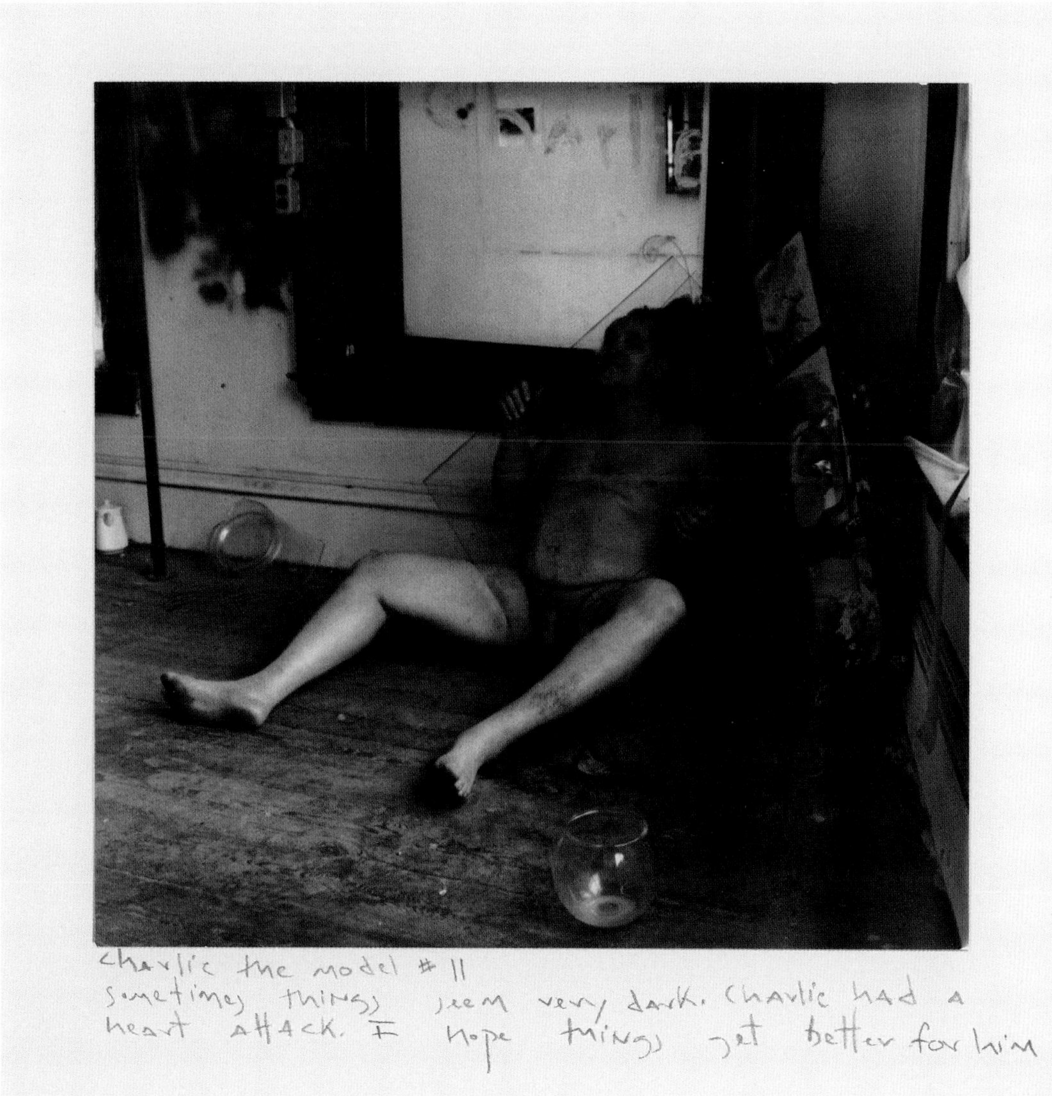

Charlie the Model #11, Providence, Rhode Island, 1976–77

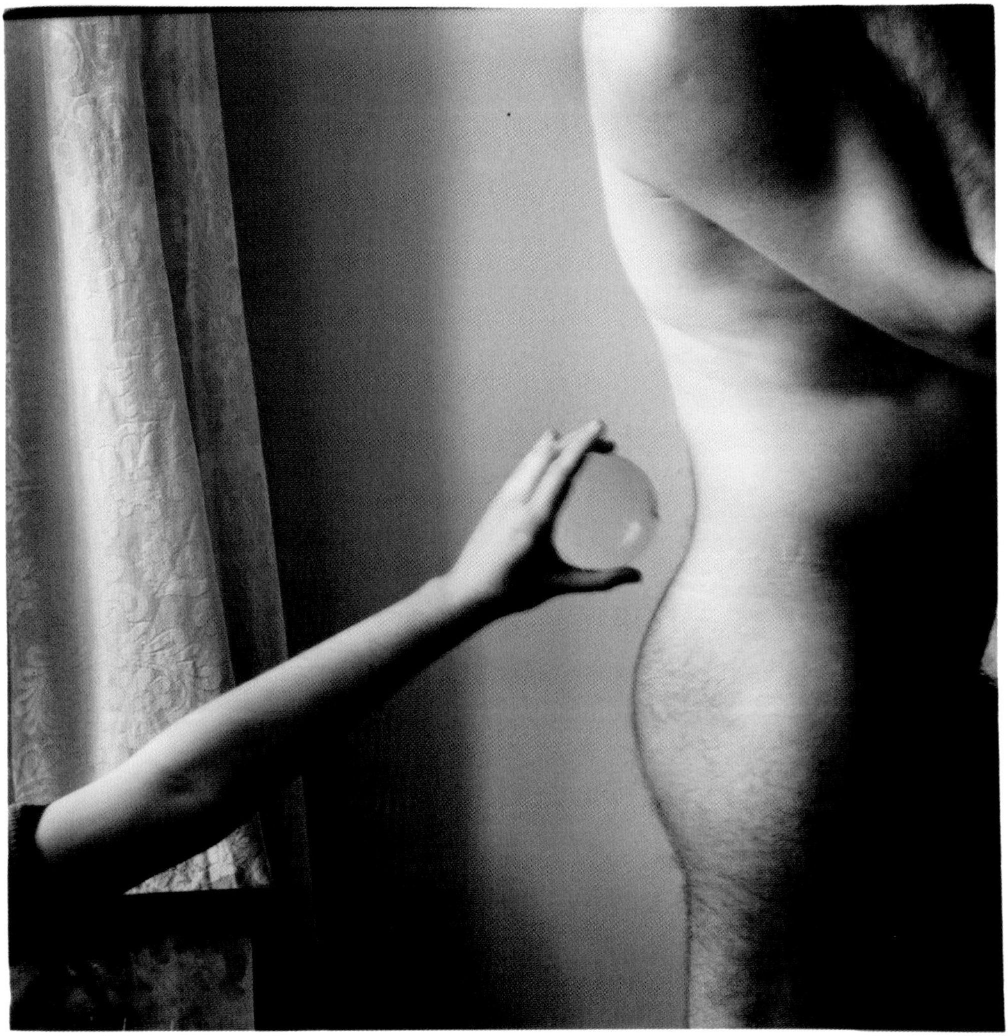

Untitled, Providence, Rhode Island, 1975–78

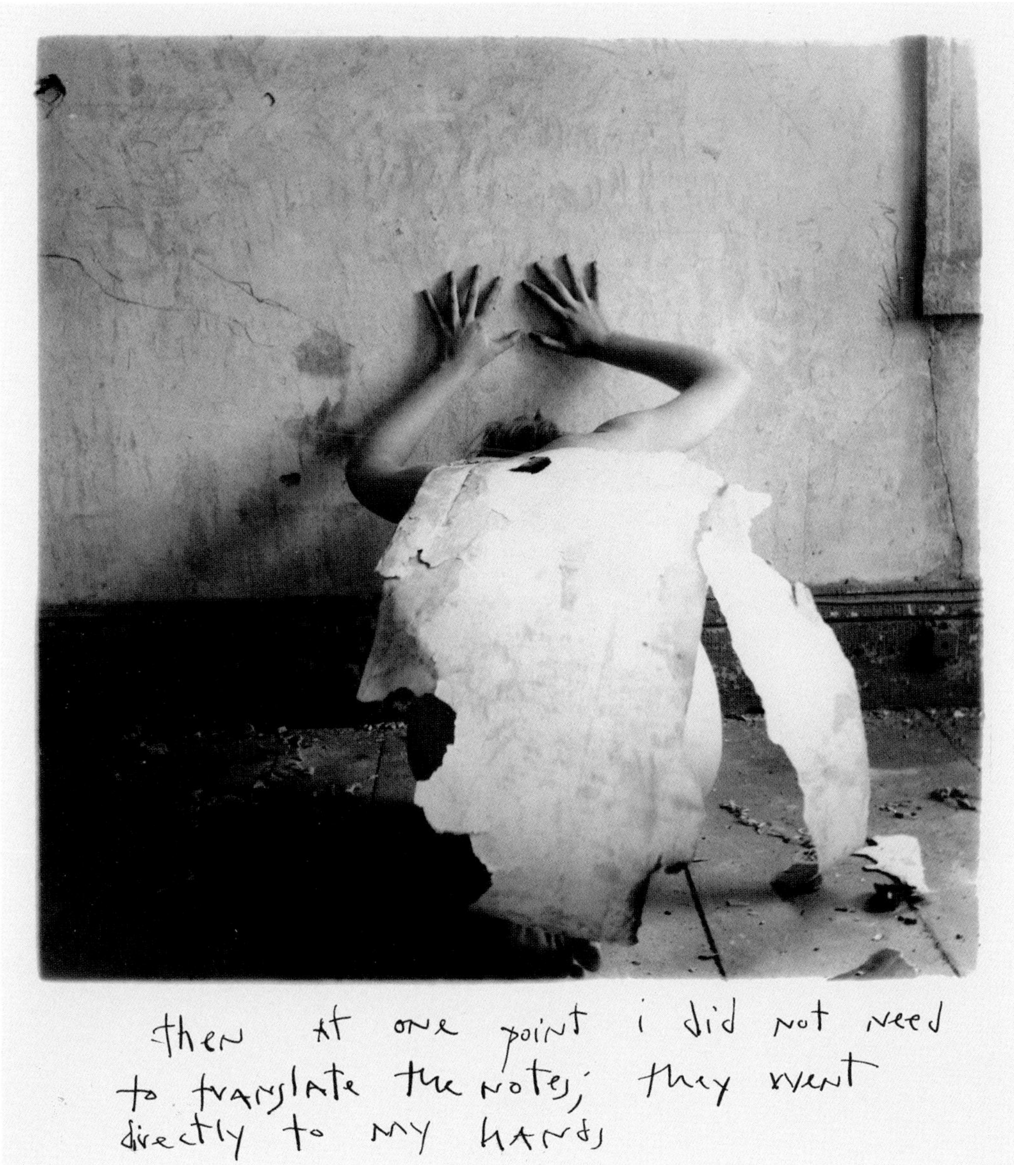

Then at one point I did not need to translate the notes; they went directly to my hands,
Providence, Rhode Island, 1976

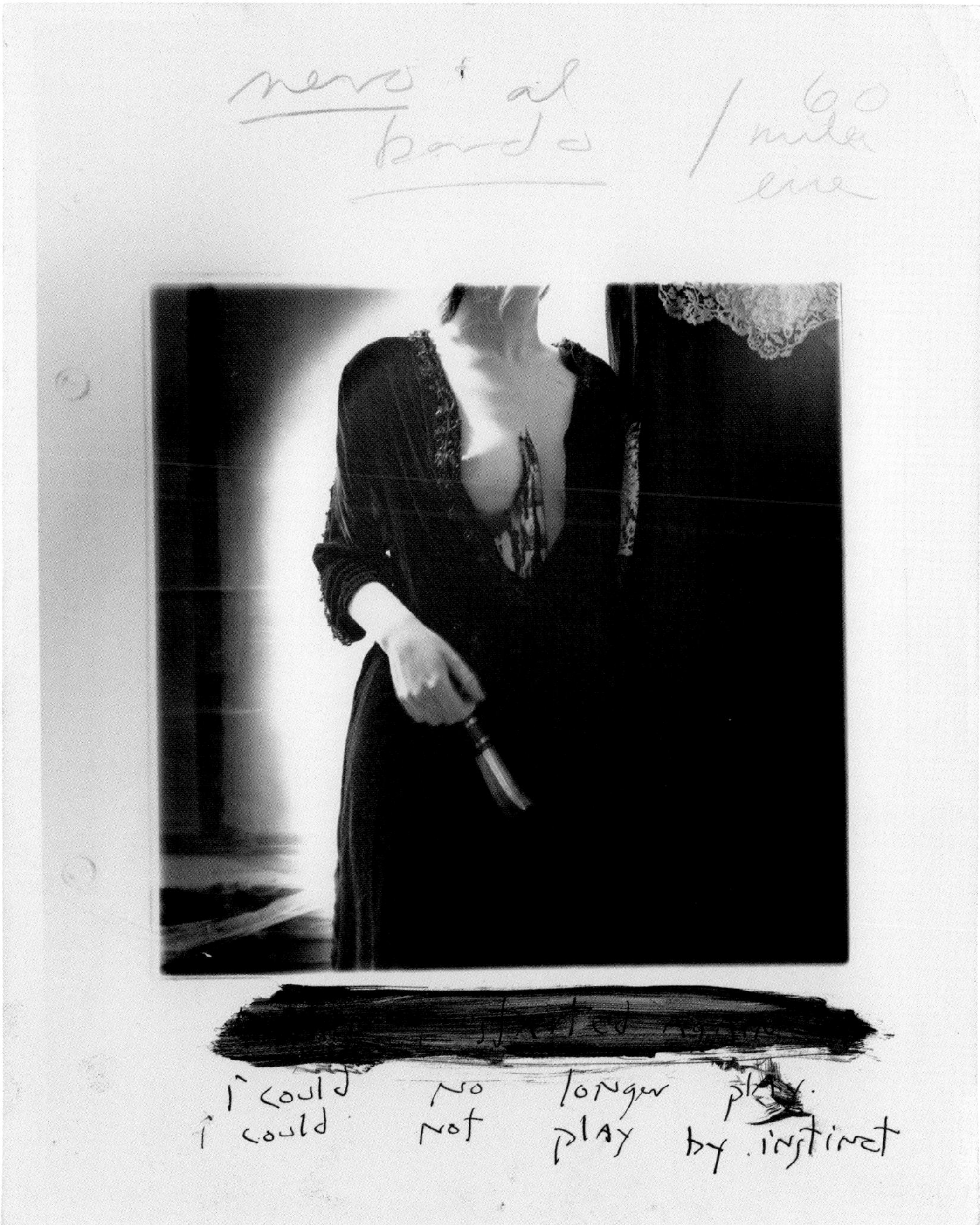

I could no longer play I could not play by instinct, Providence, Rhode Island, 1977

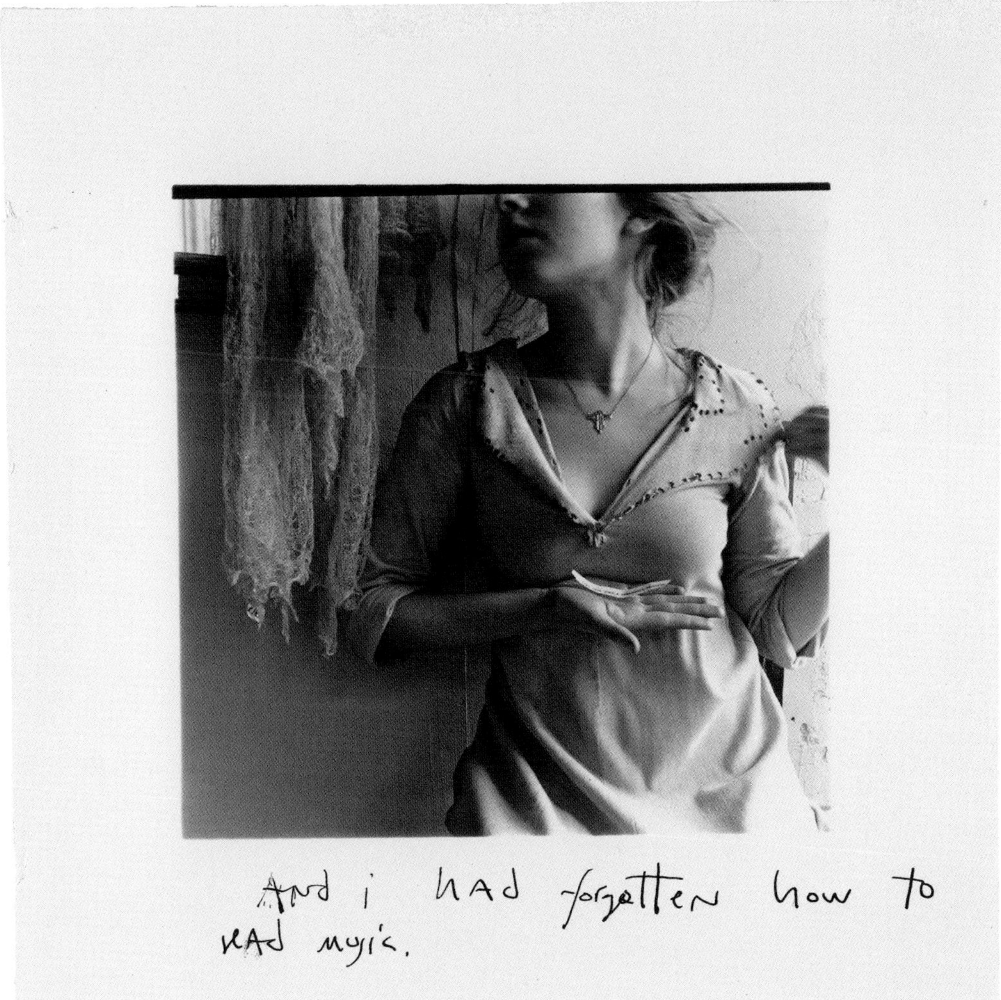

And I had forgotten how to read music, Providence, Rhode Island, 1976

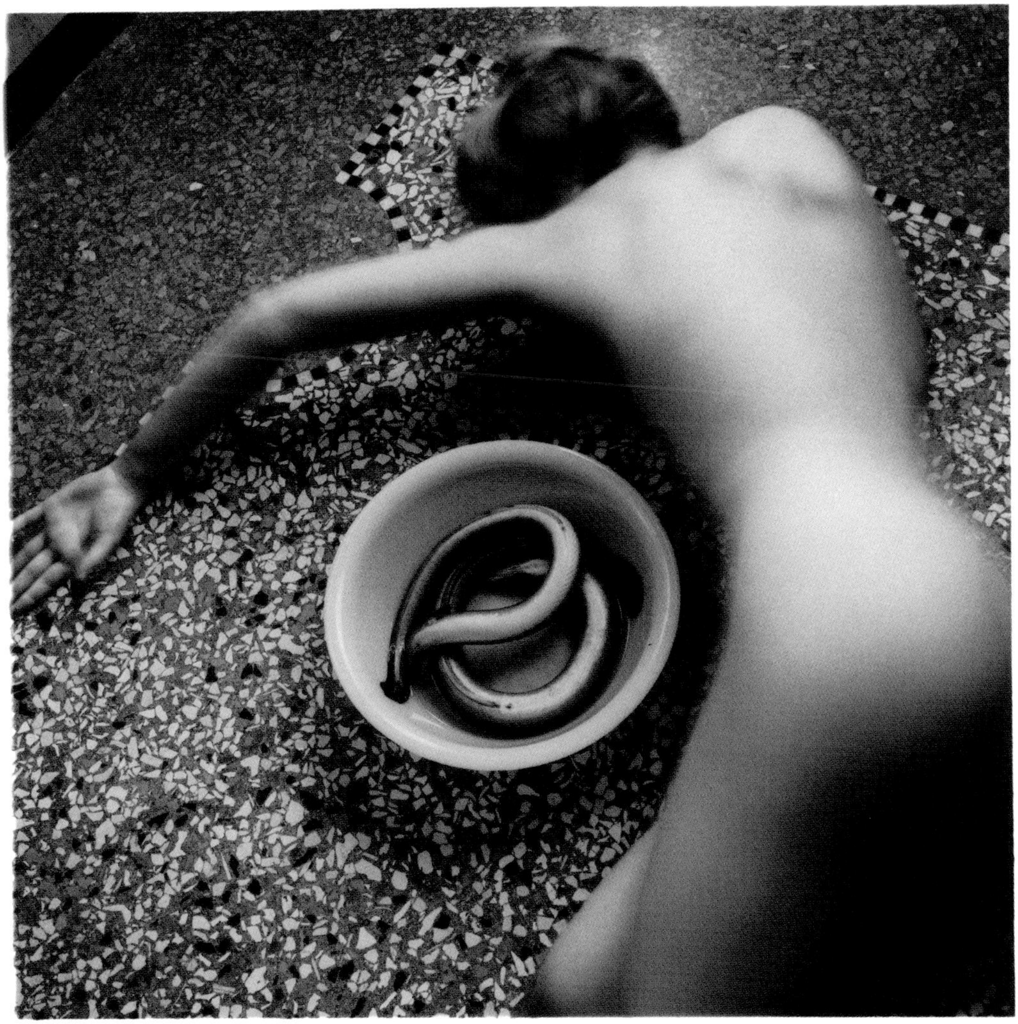

From Eel series, Venice, Italy, 1978

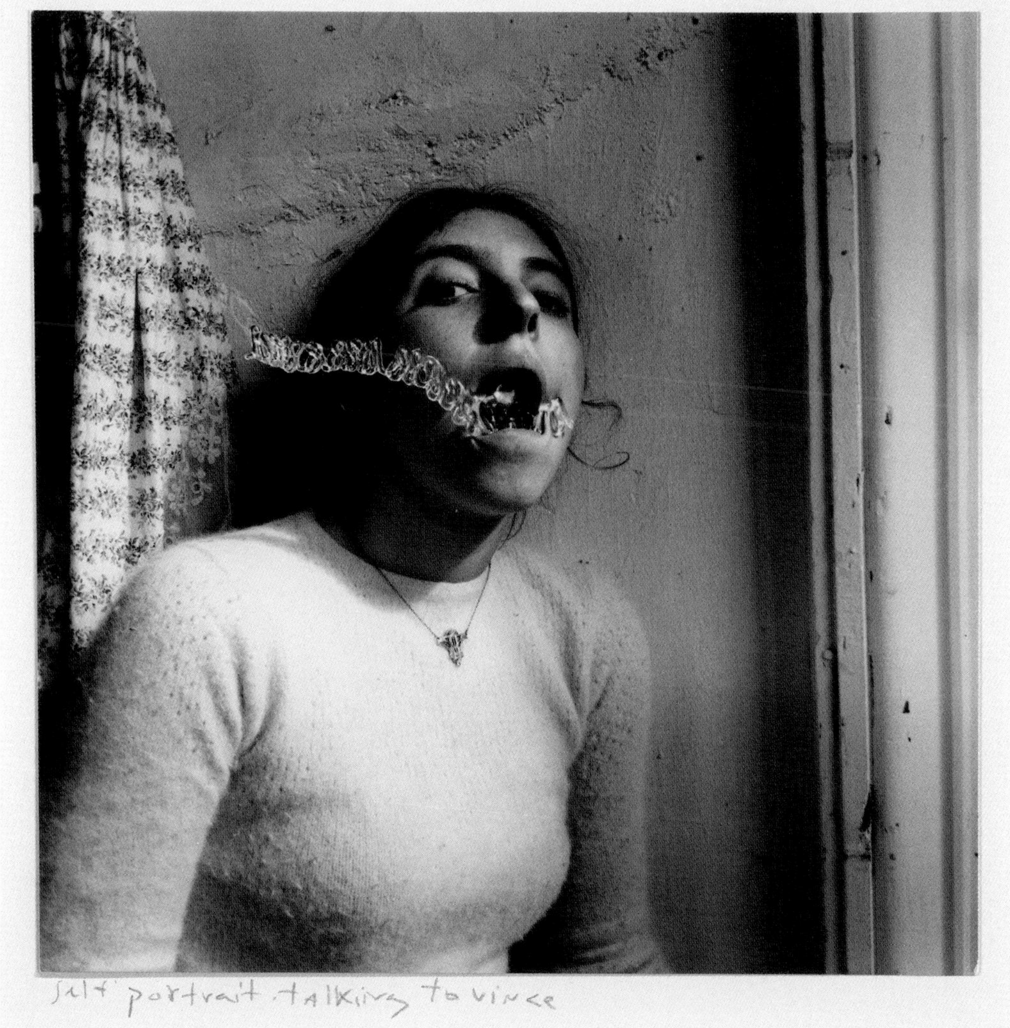

Self-portrait talking to Vince, Providence, Rhode Island, 1977

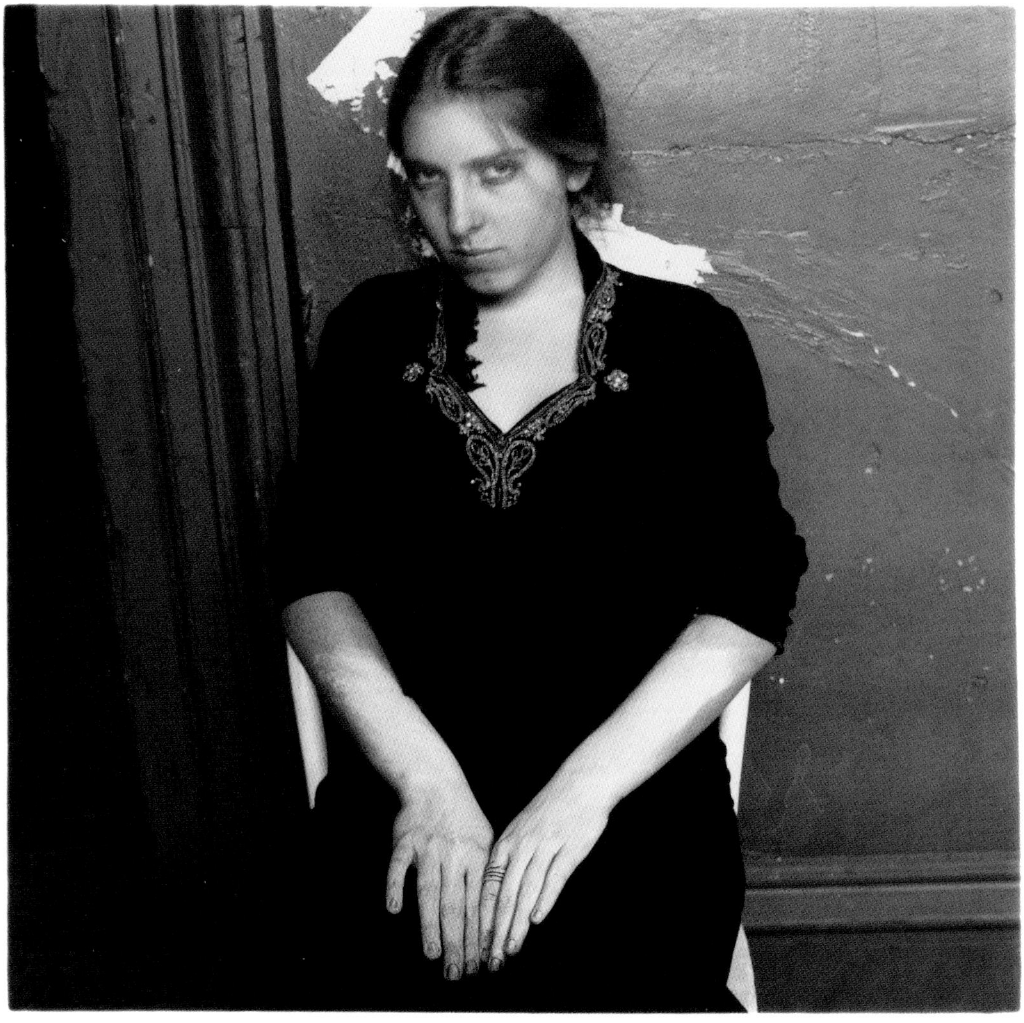

Untitled, New York, 1979–80

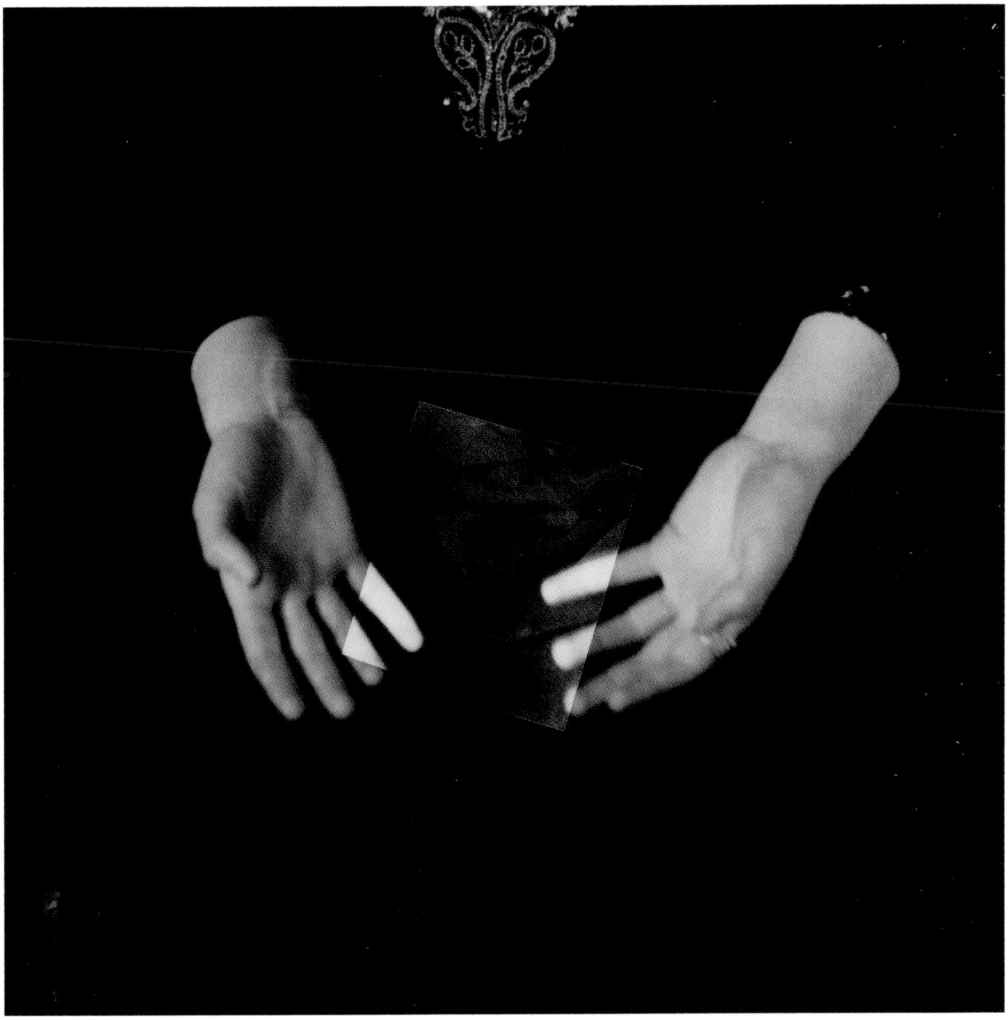

Untitled, New York, 1979–80

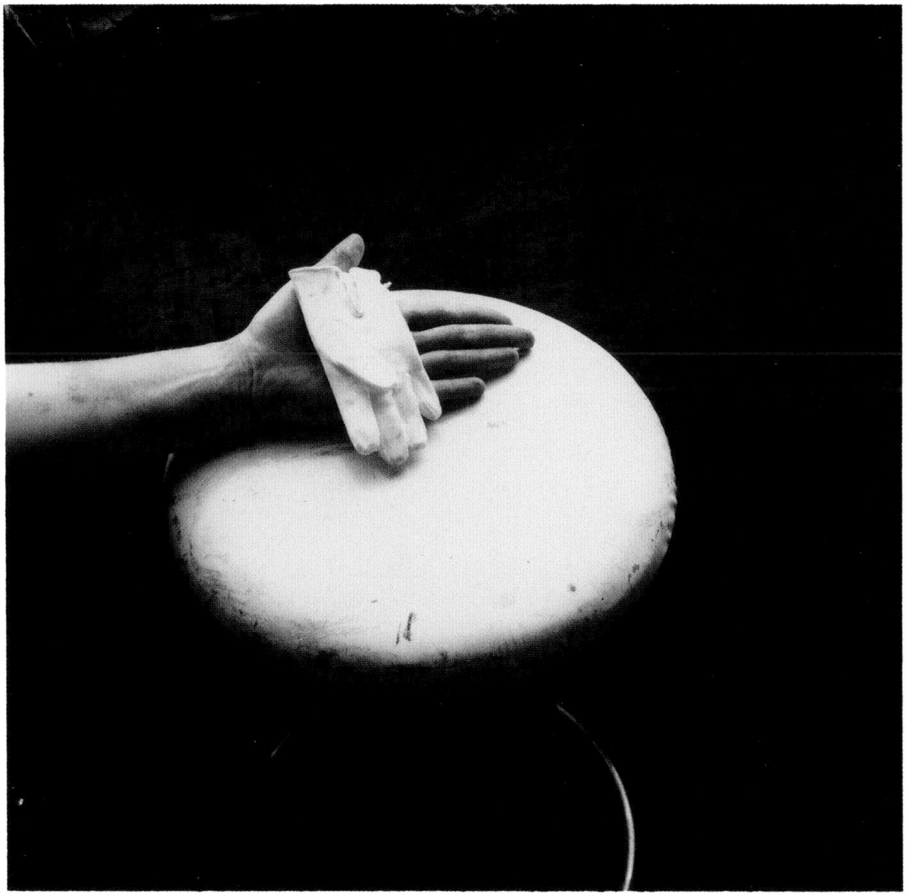

Untitled, Rome, Italy, 1977–78

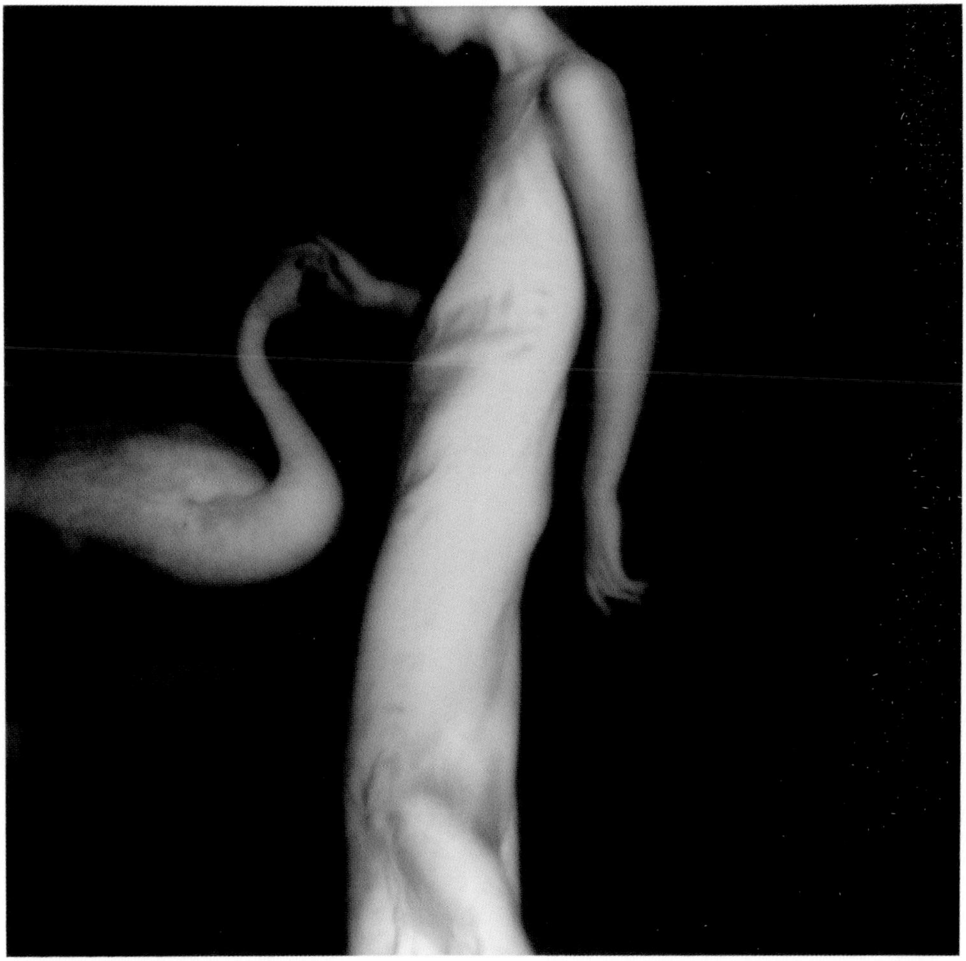

Untitled, Providence, Rhode Island, 1975–78

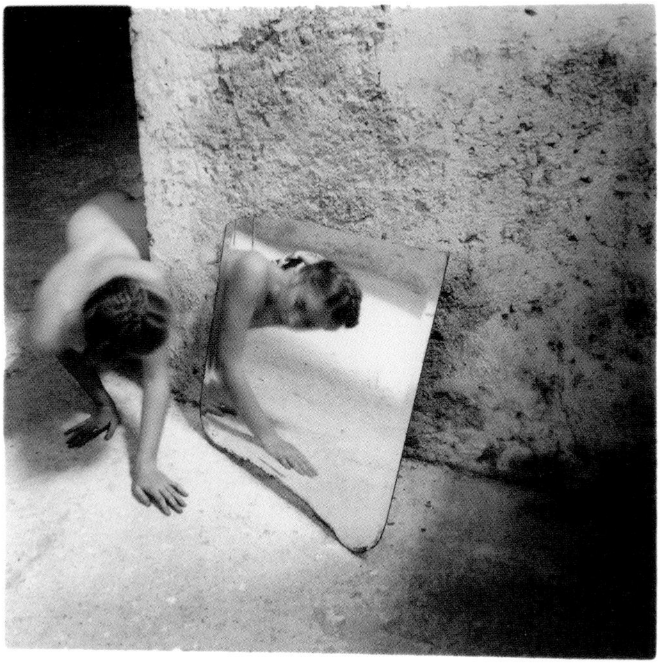

Self-deceit #1, Rome, Italy, 1978

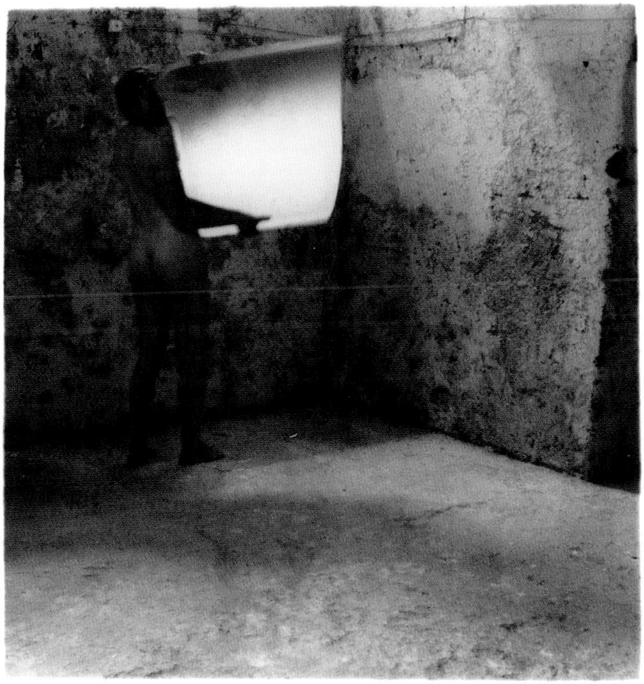

Self-deceit #2, Rome, Italy, 1978

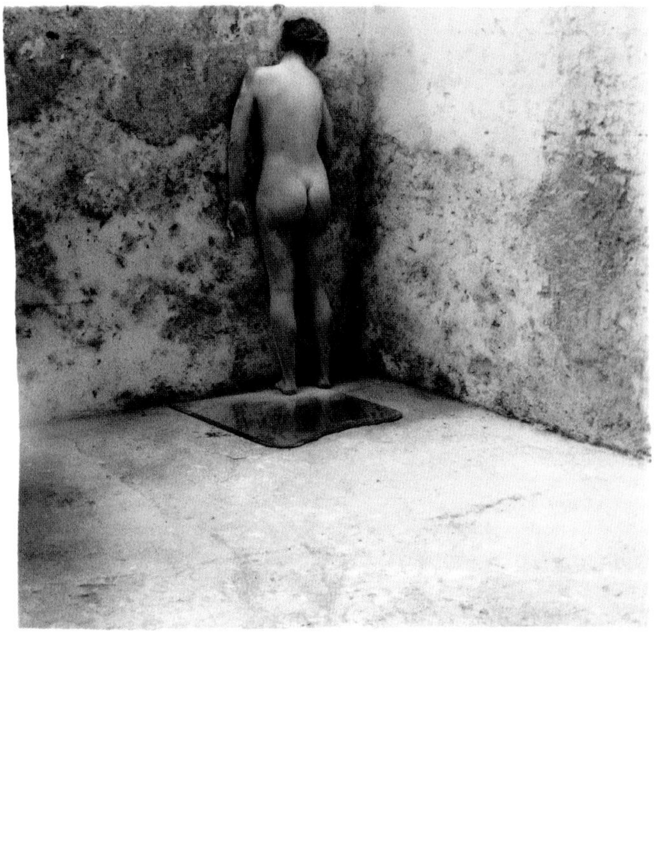

Self-deceit #3, Rome, Italy, 1978

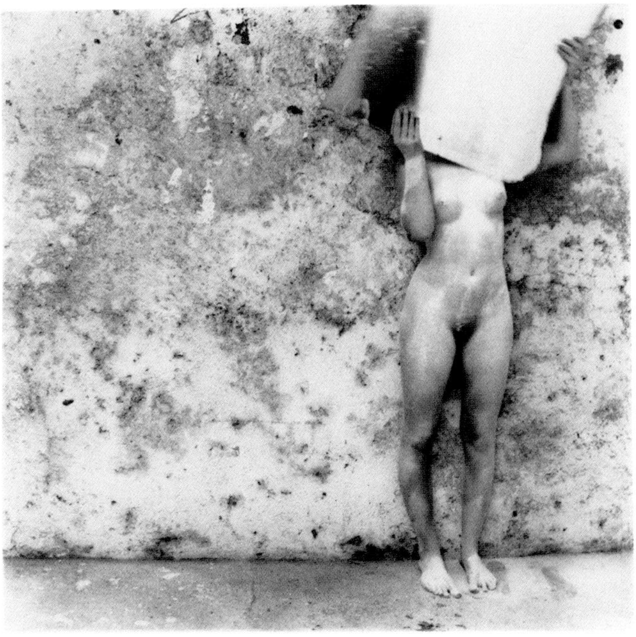

Self-deceit #4, Rome, Italy, 1978

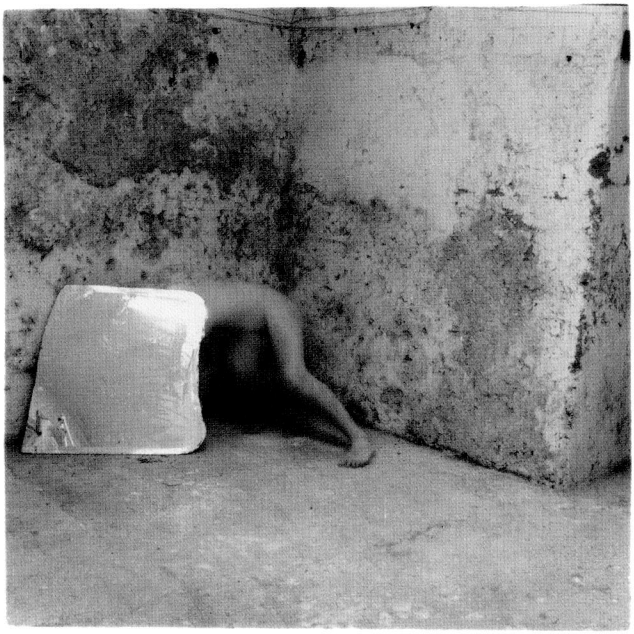

Self-deceit #5, Rome, Italy, 1978

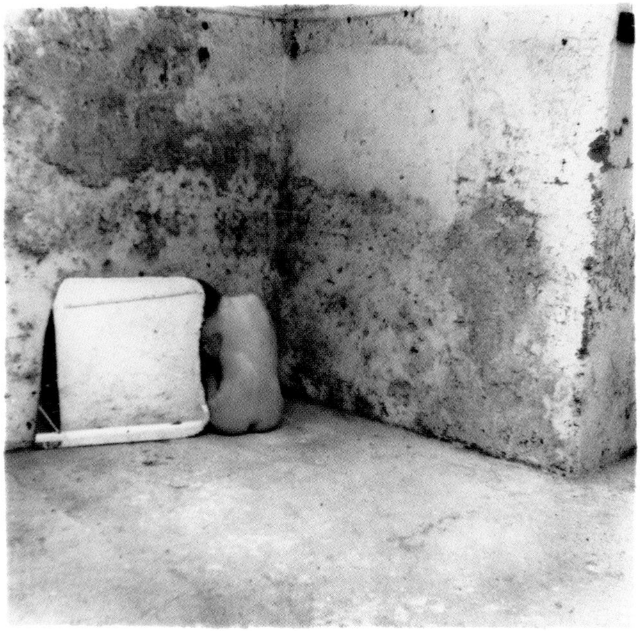

Self-deceit #6, Rome, Italy, 1978

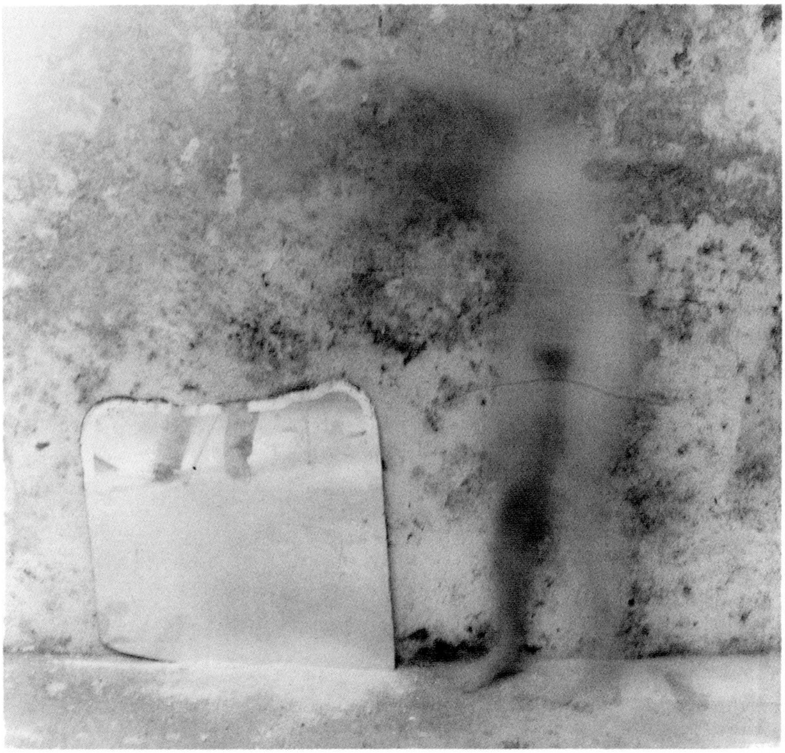

Self-deceit #7, Rome, Italy, 1978

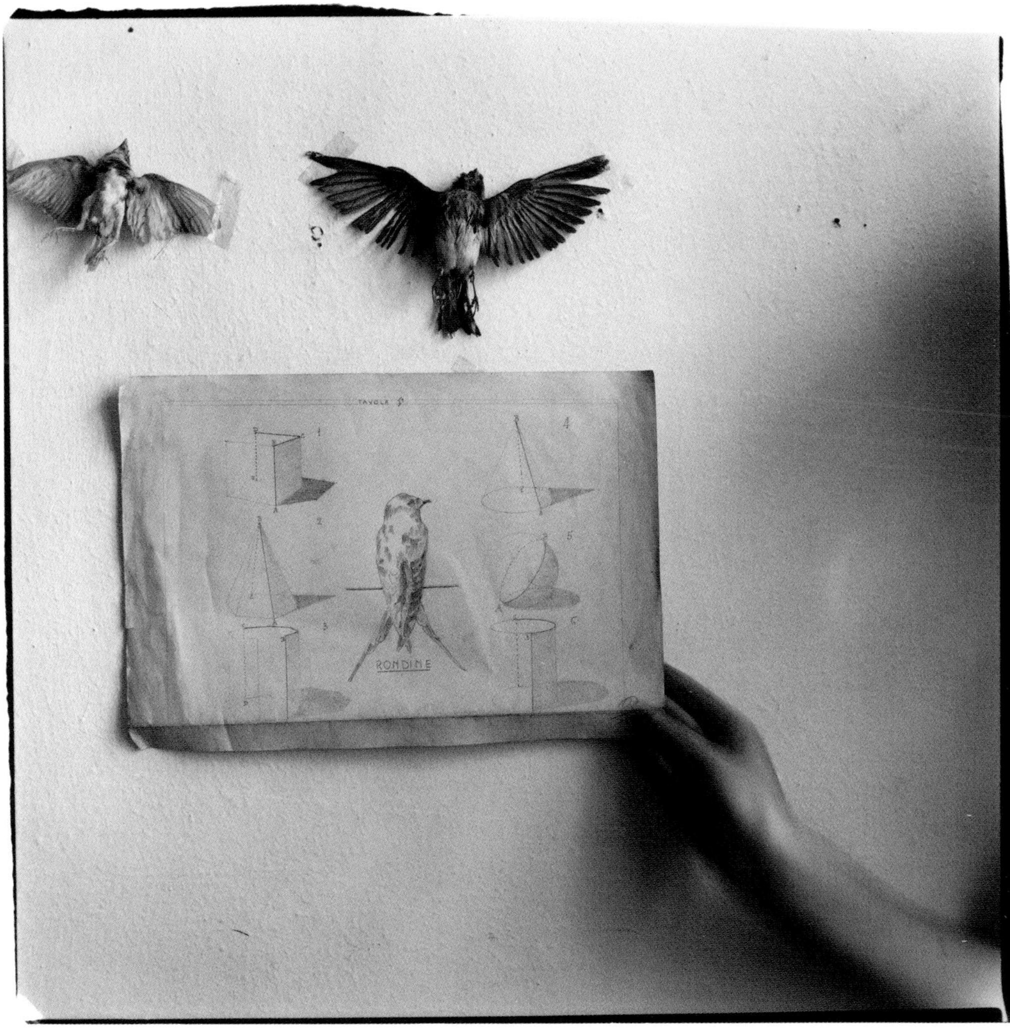

Untitled, Rome, Italy, 1977–78

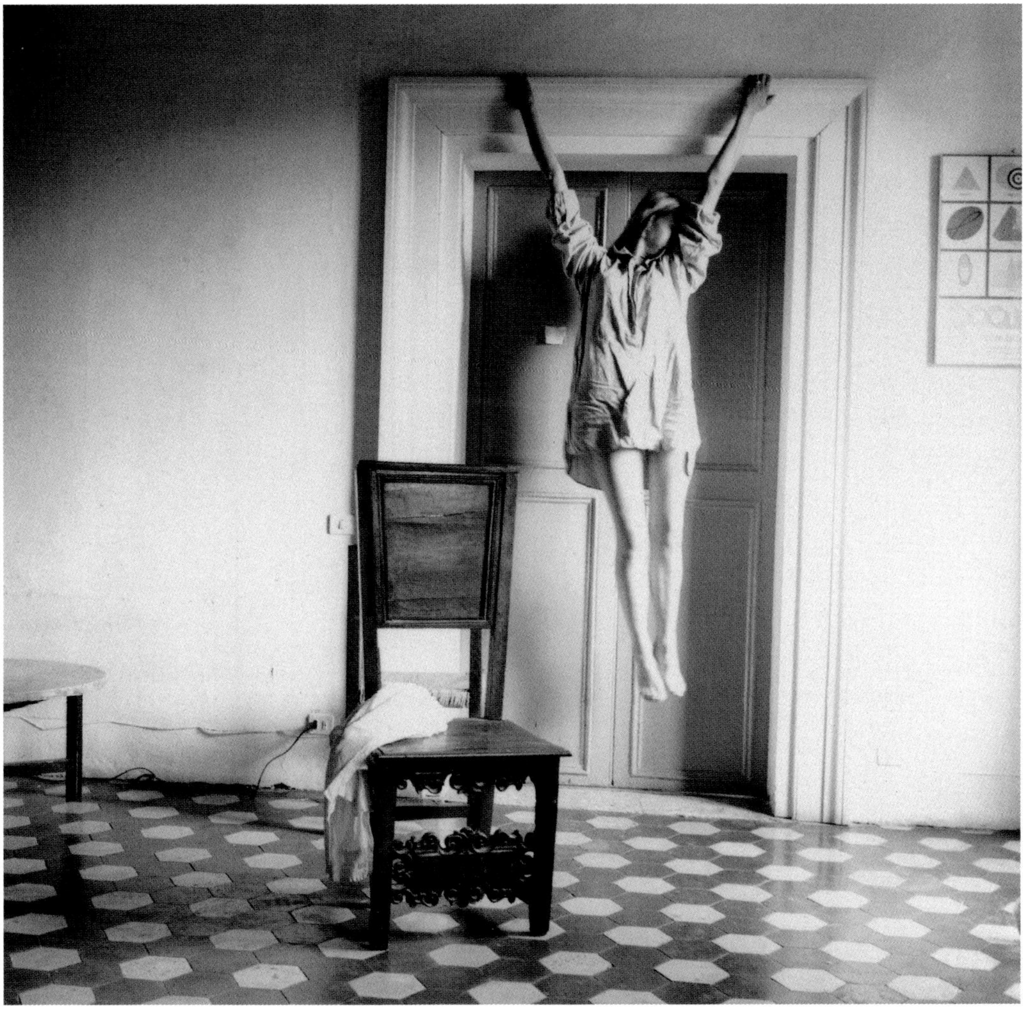

Untitled, Rome, Italy, 1977–78

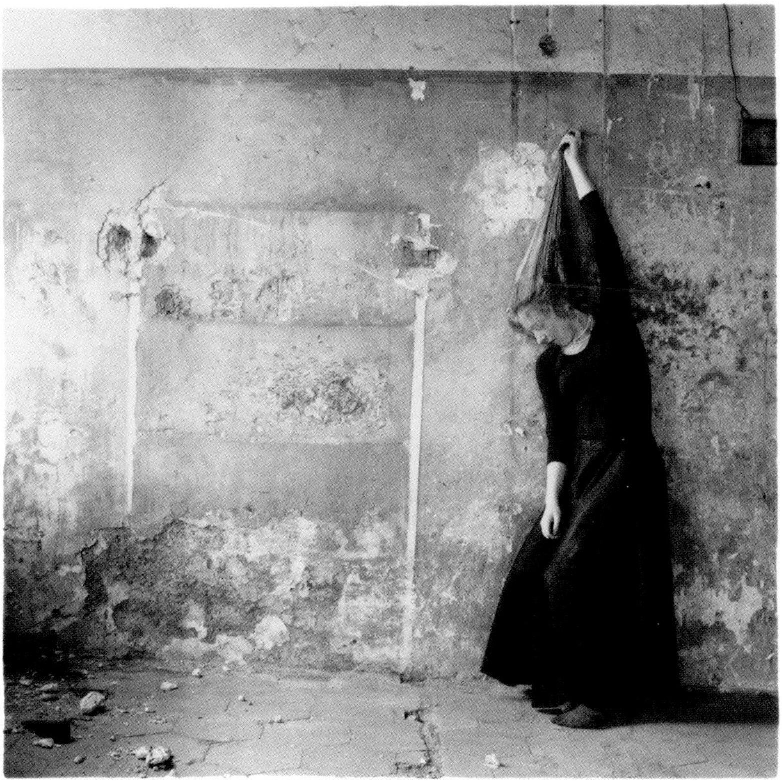

Untitled, Rome, Italy, 1977–78

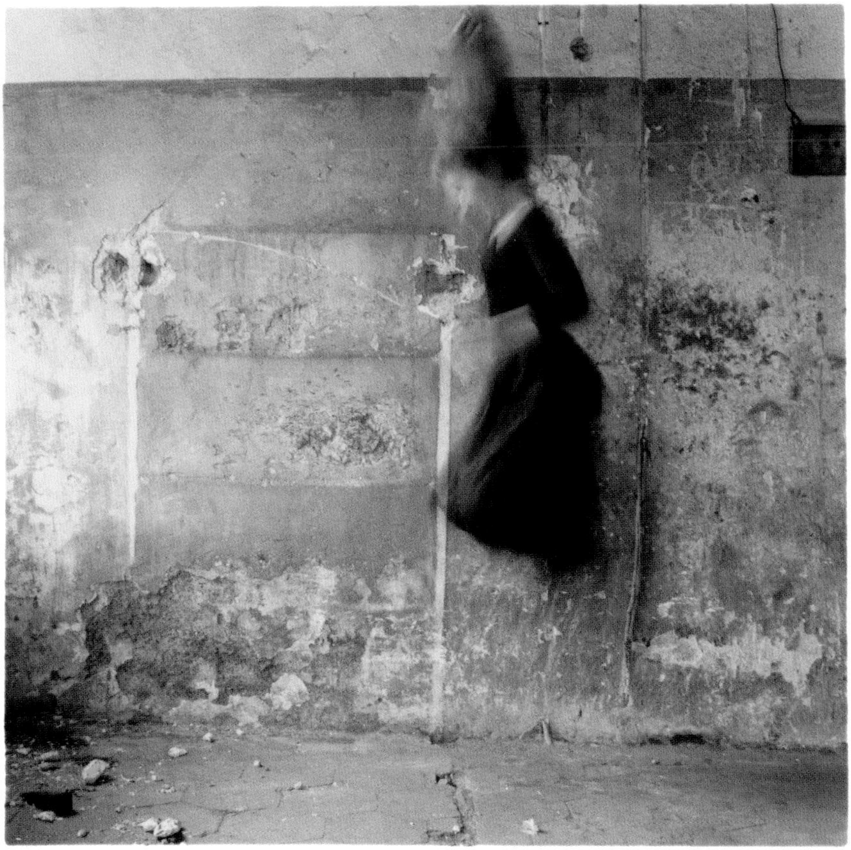

Untitled, Rome, Italy, 1977–78

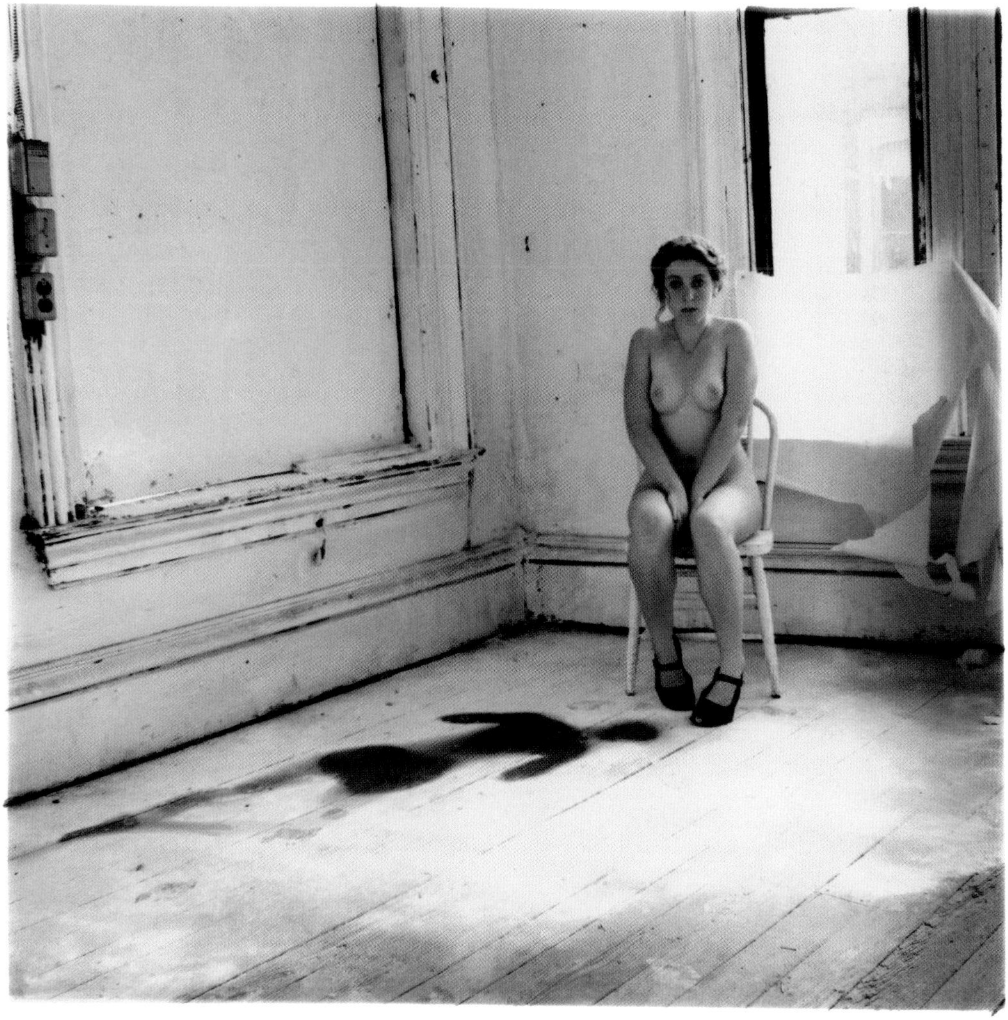

 Untitled, Providence, Rhode Island, 1976

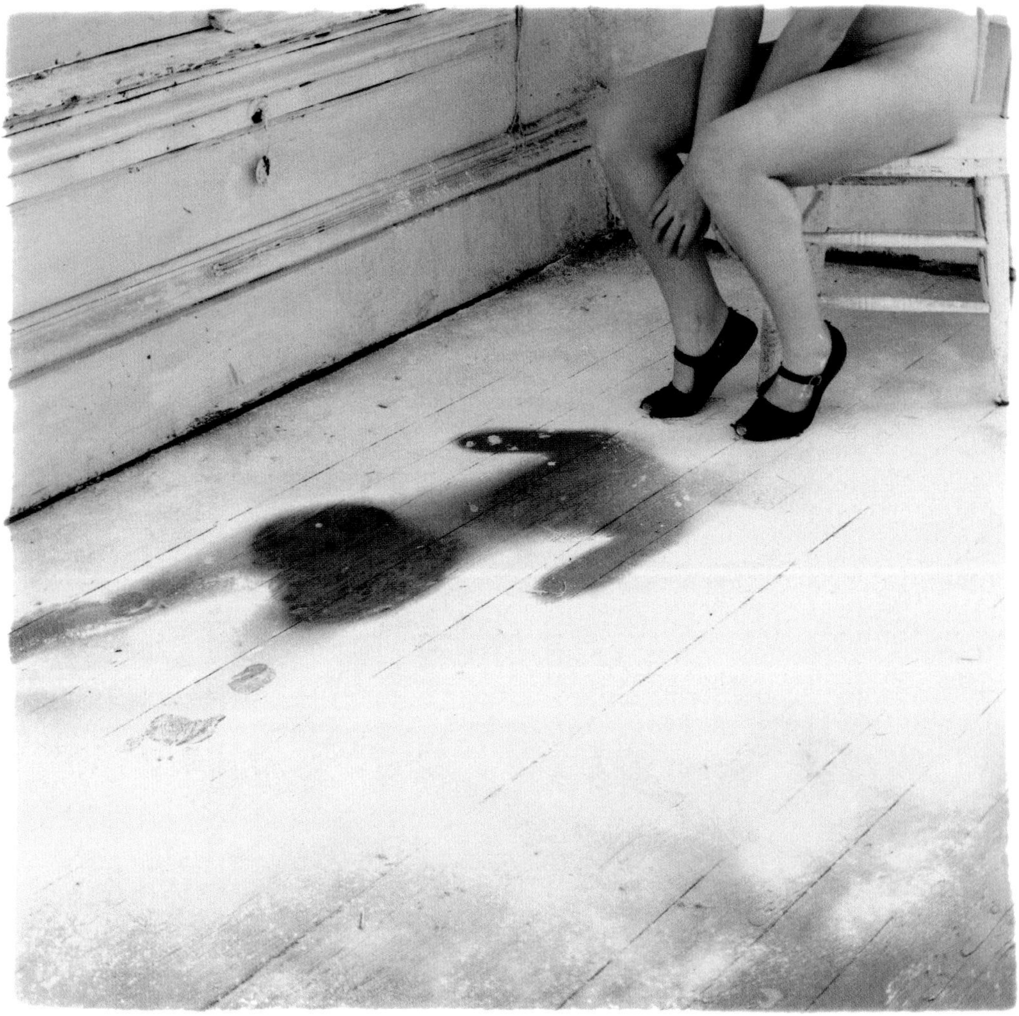

Untitled, Providence, Rhode Island, 1976

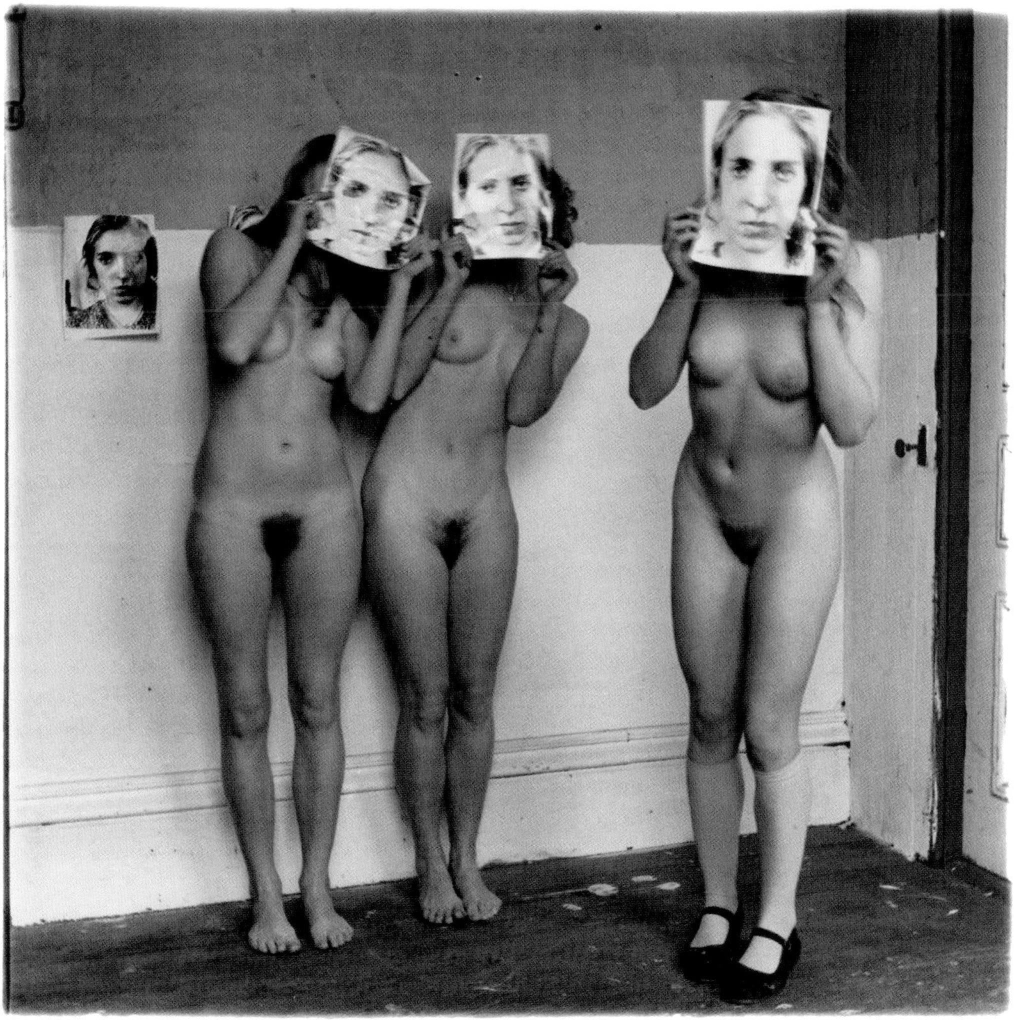

About Being My Model, Providence, Rhode Island, 1976

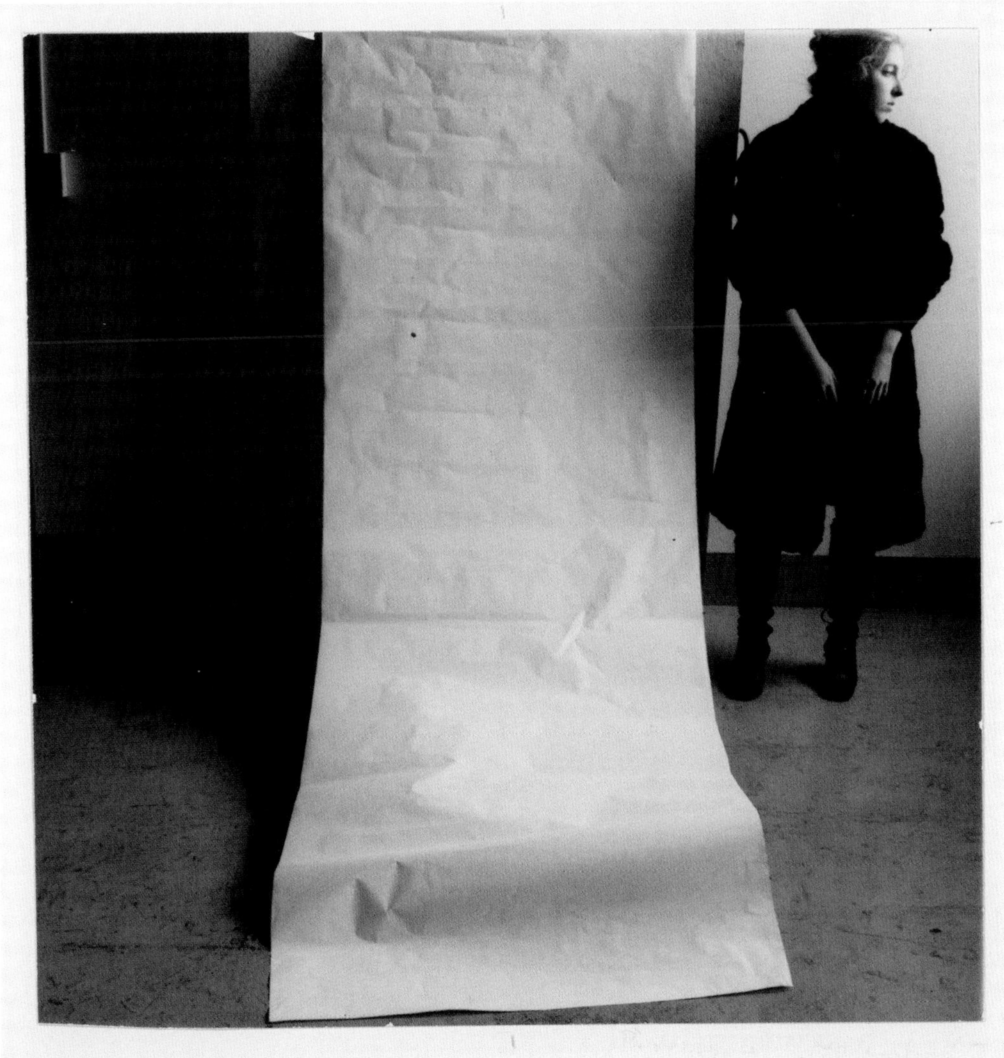

Spring in Providence #1, Providence, Rhode Island, 1976

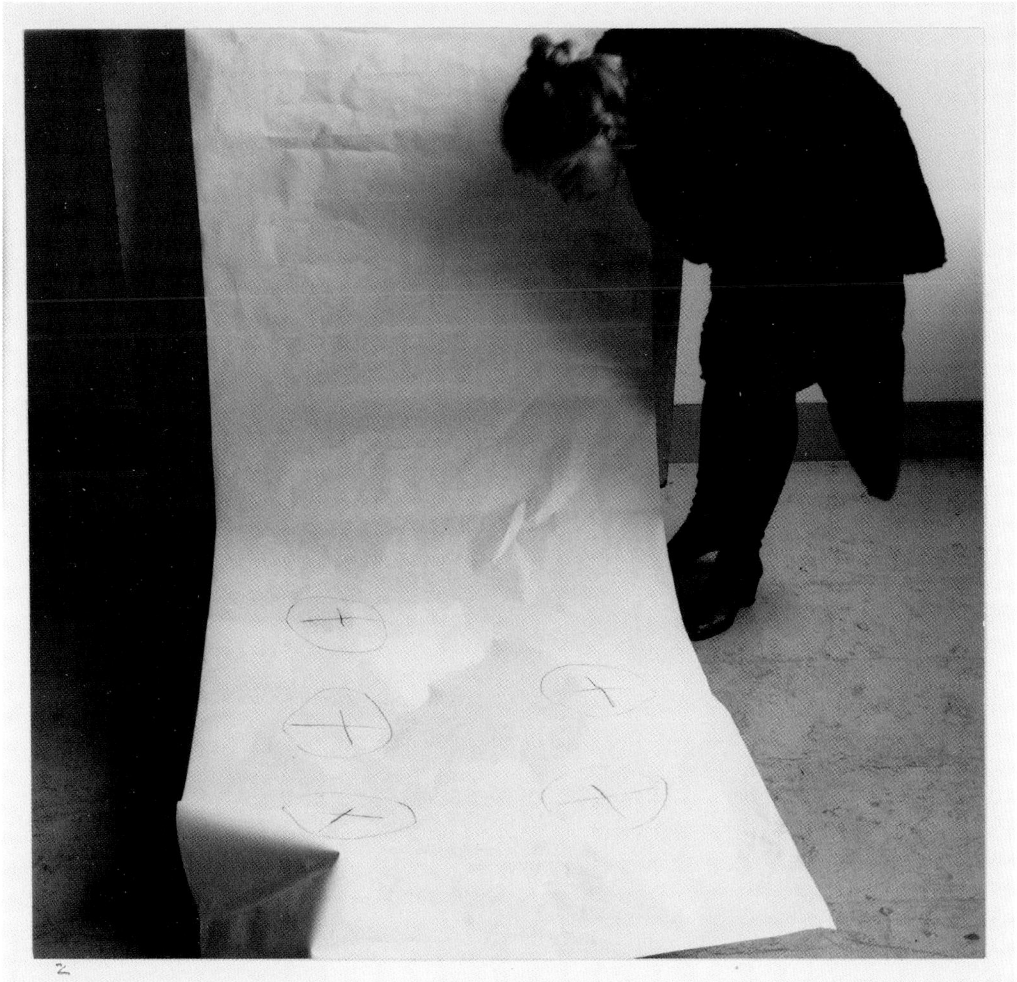

Spring in Providence #2, Providence, Rhode Island, 1976

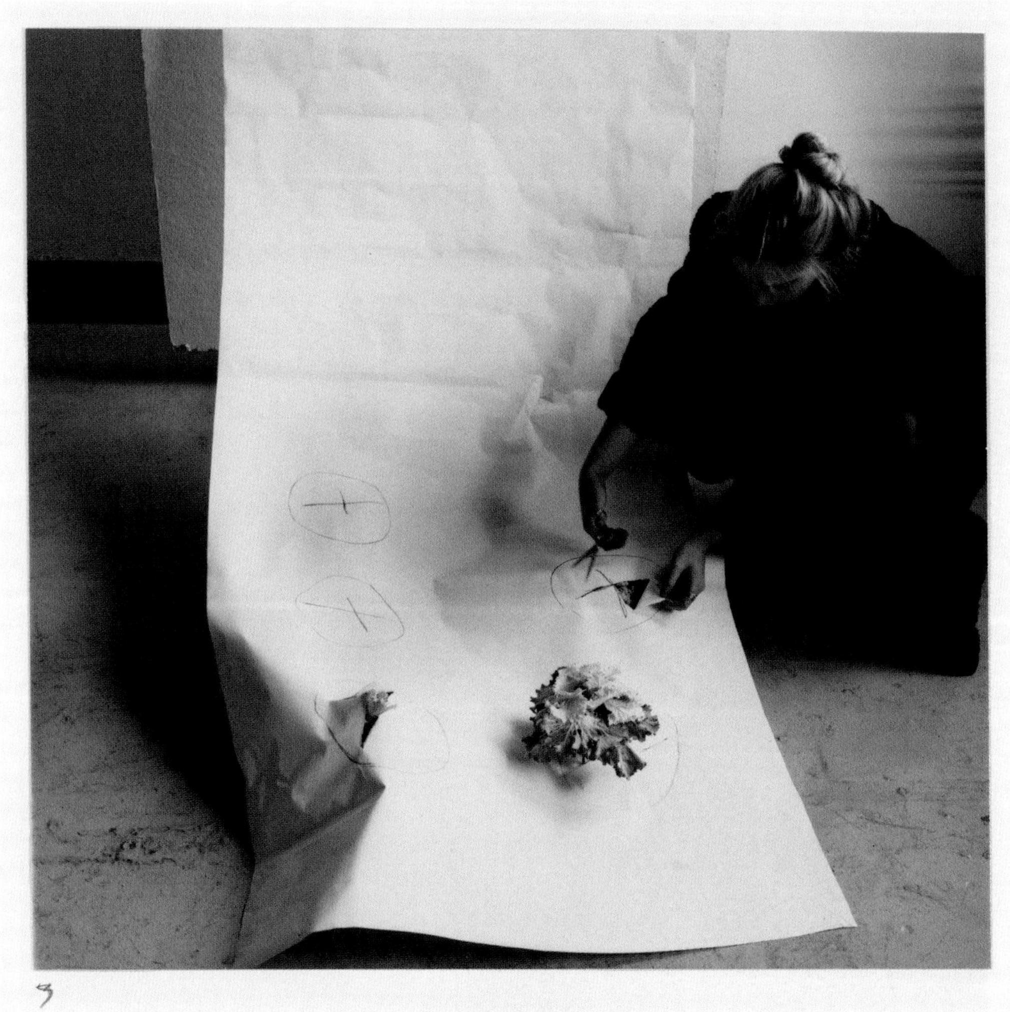

Spring in Providence #3, Providence, Rhode Island, 1976

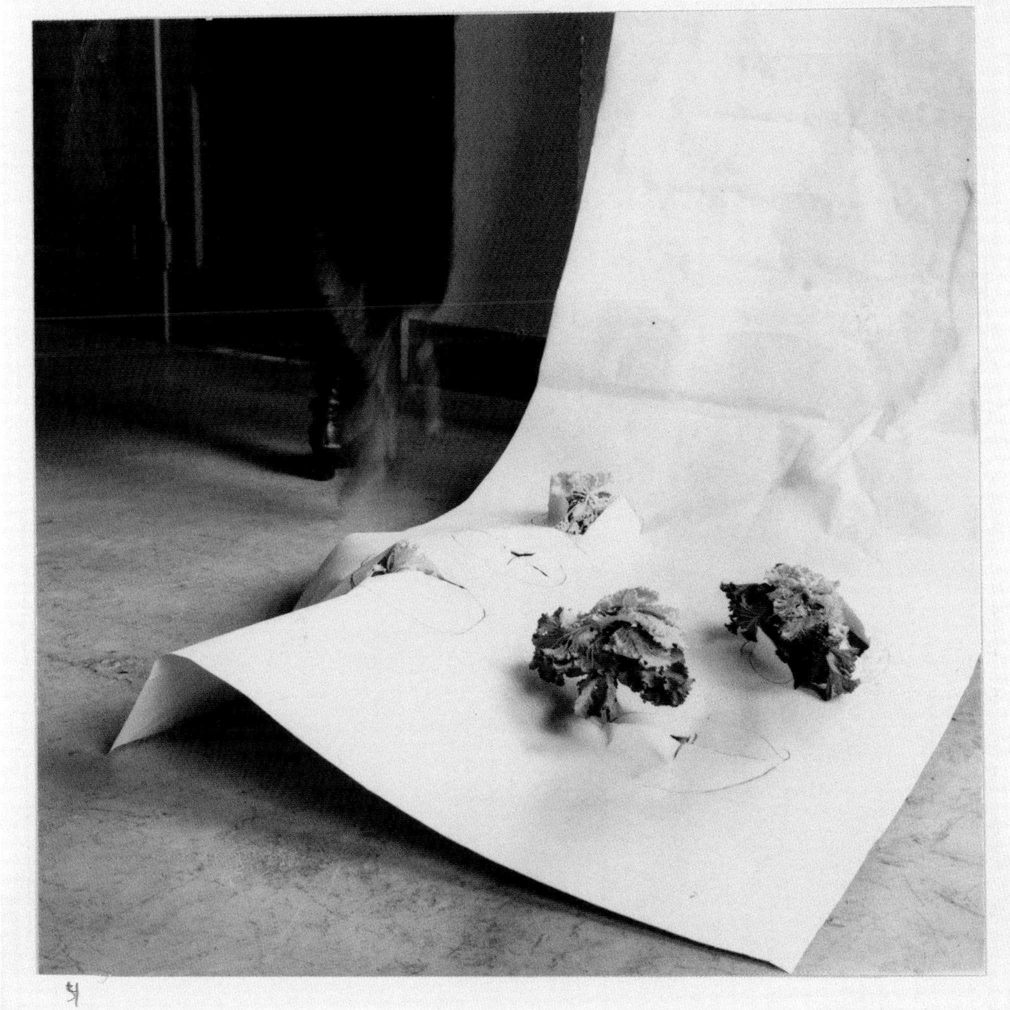

 Spring in Providence #4, Providence, Rhode Island, 1976

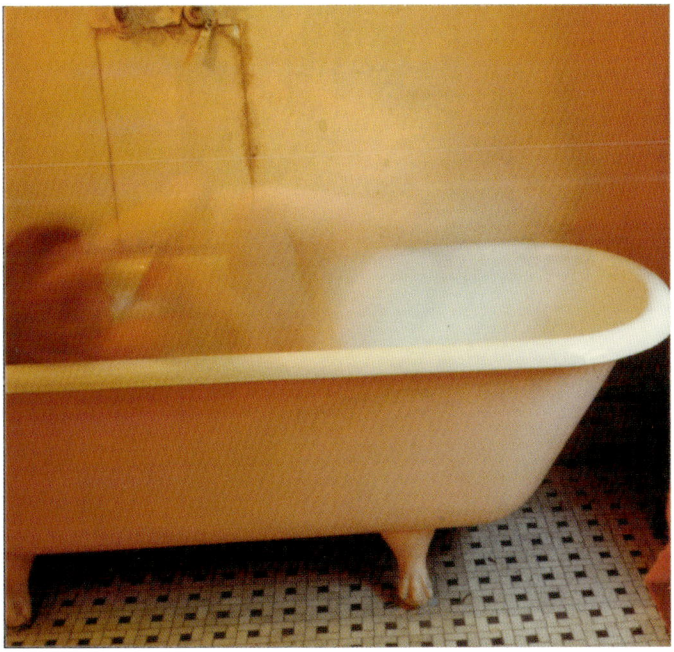

Untitled, New York, 1979

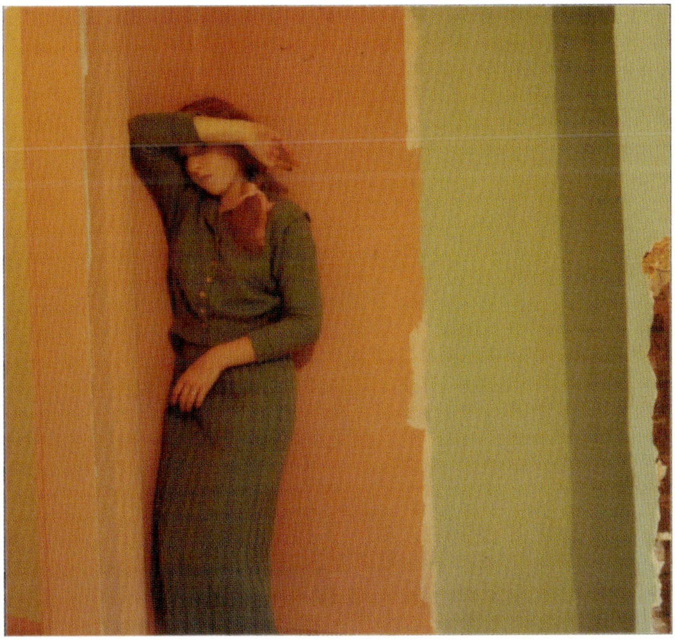

Untitled, New York, 1979

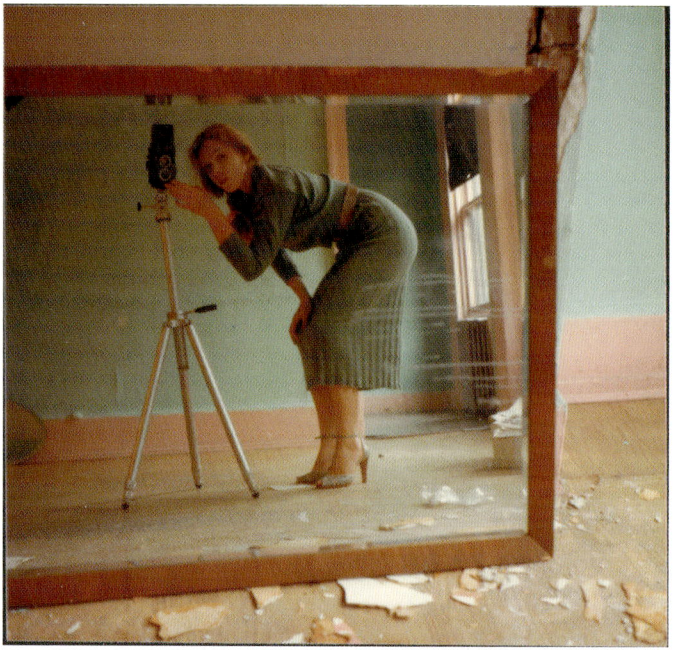

Untitled, New York, 1979

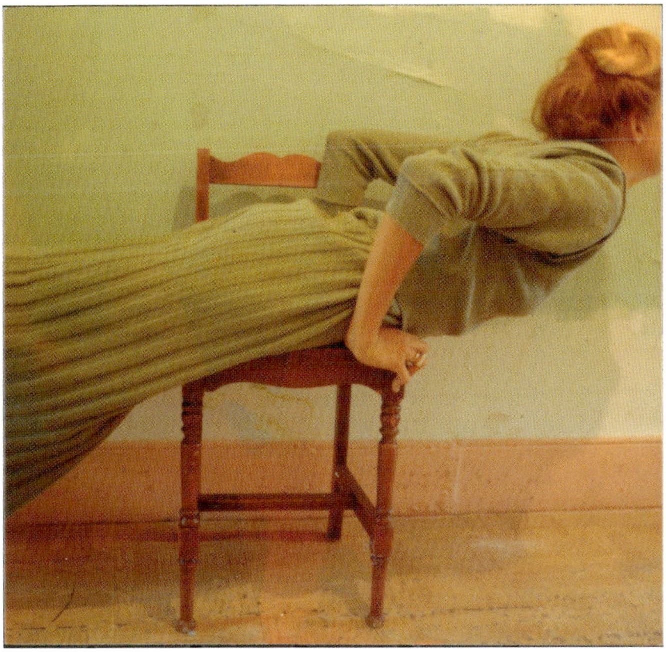

Untitled, New York, 1979

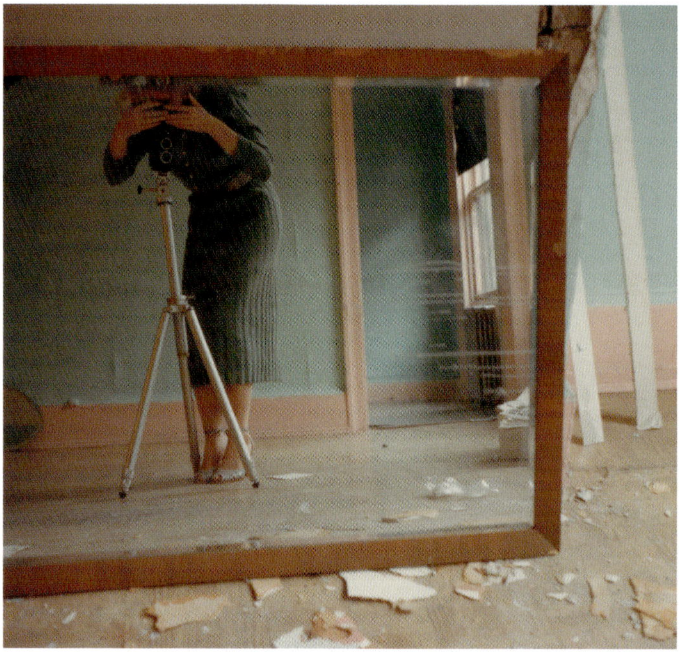

Untitled, New York, 1979

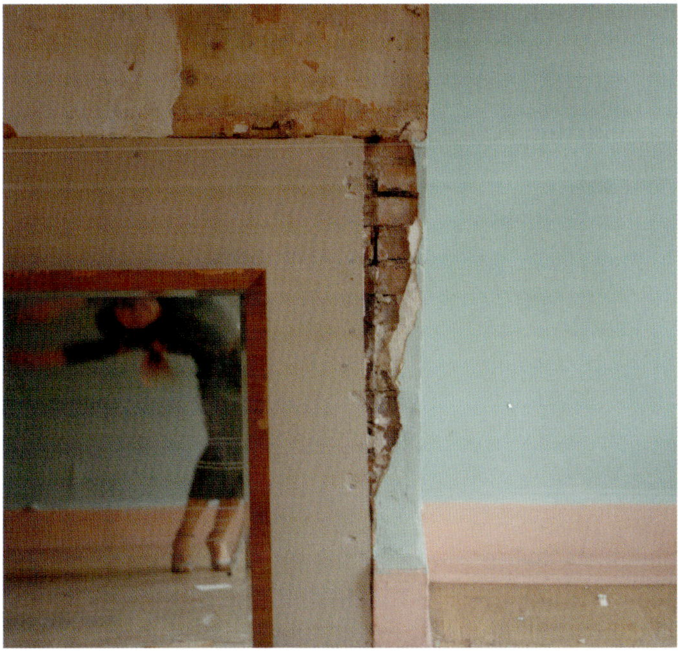

 Untitled, New York, 1979

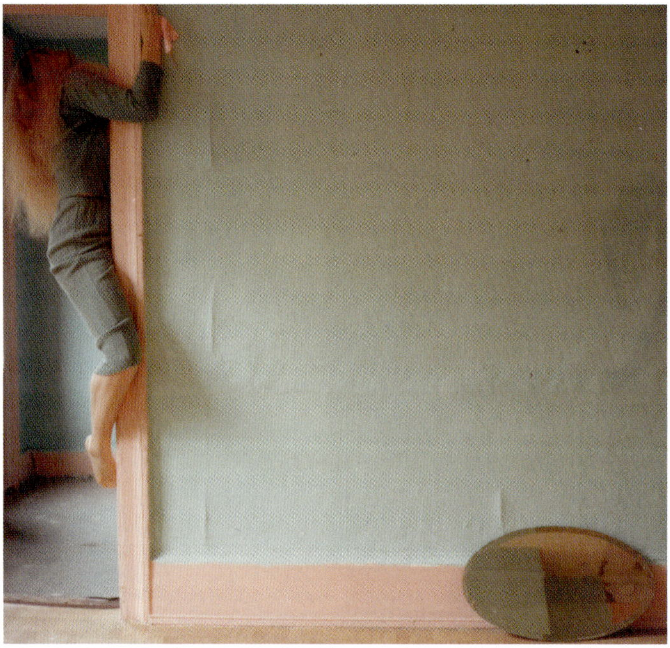

Untitled, New York, 1979

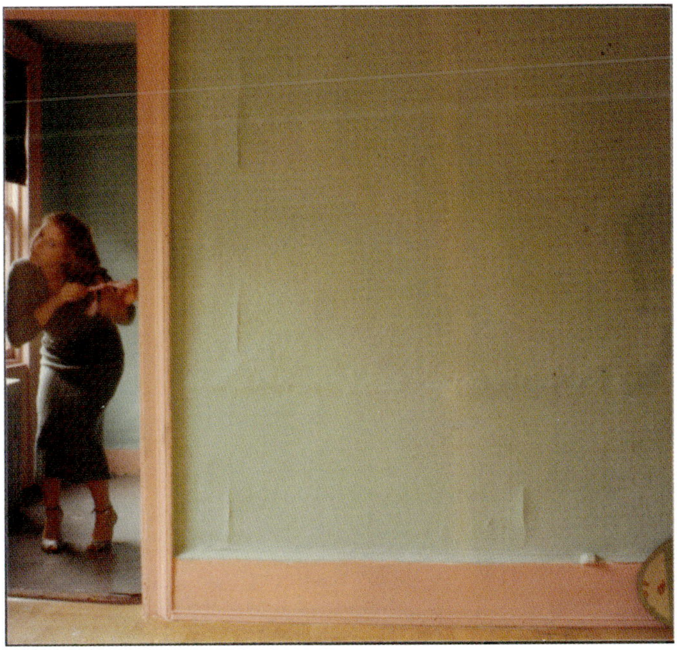

Untitled, New York, 1979–80

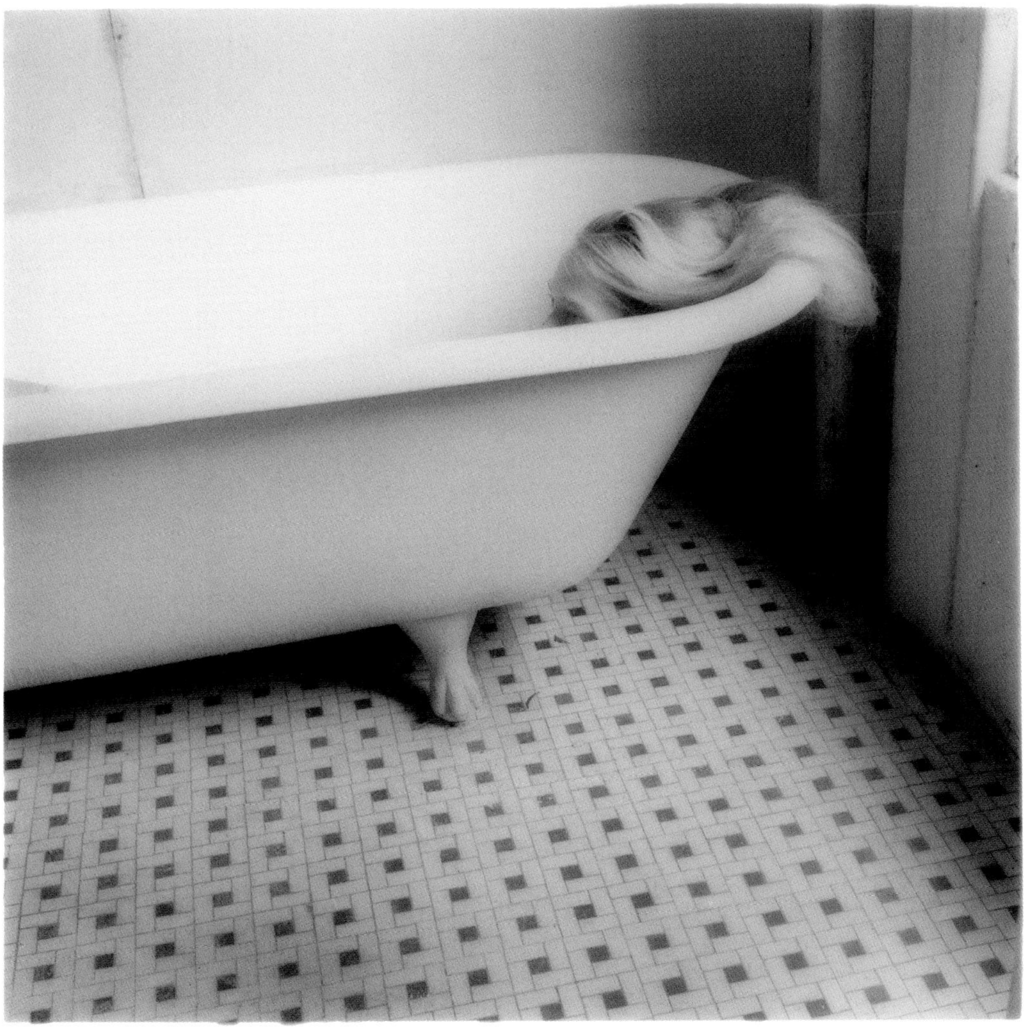

Untitled, New York, 1979–80

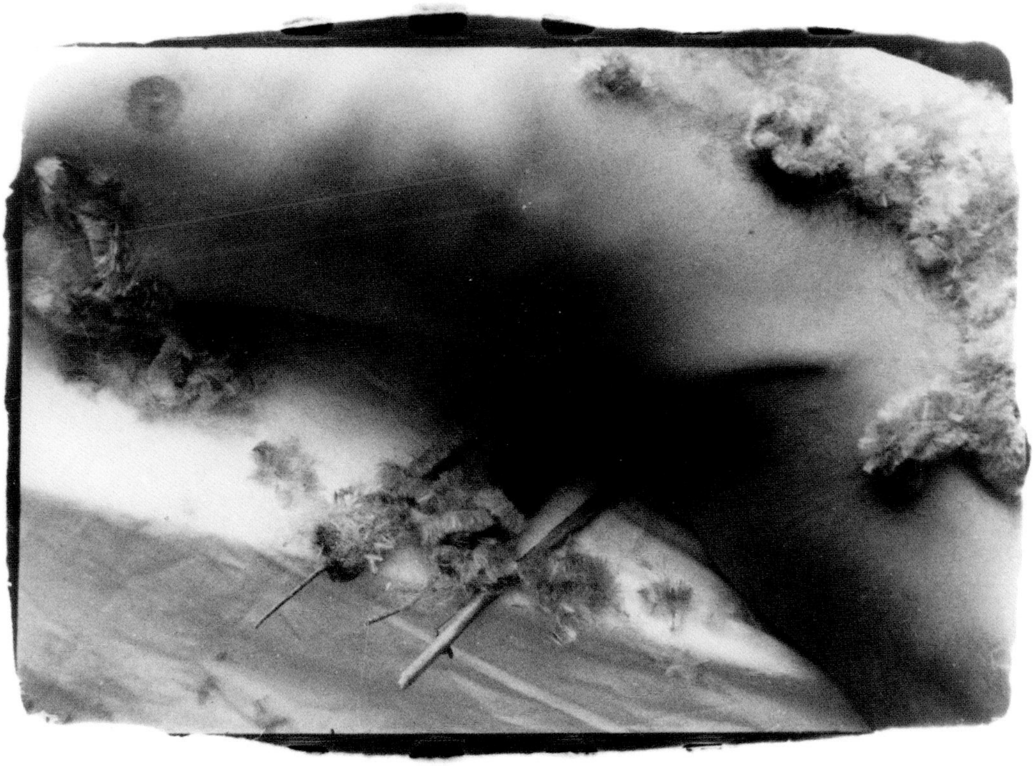

 Untitled, MacDowell/Stanwood, 1979–80

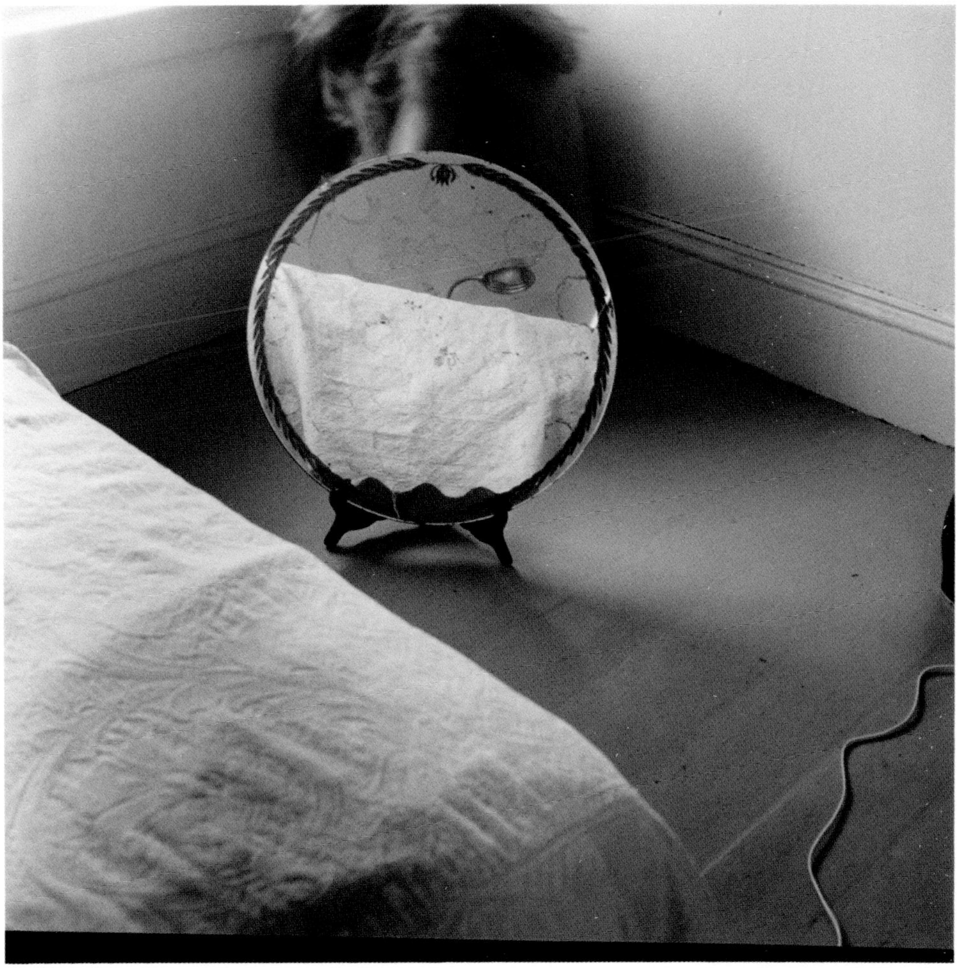

Untitled, New York, 1979–80

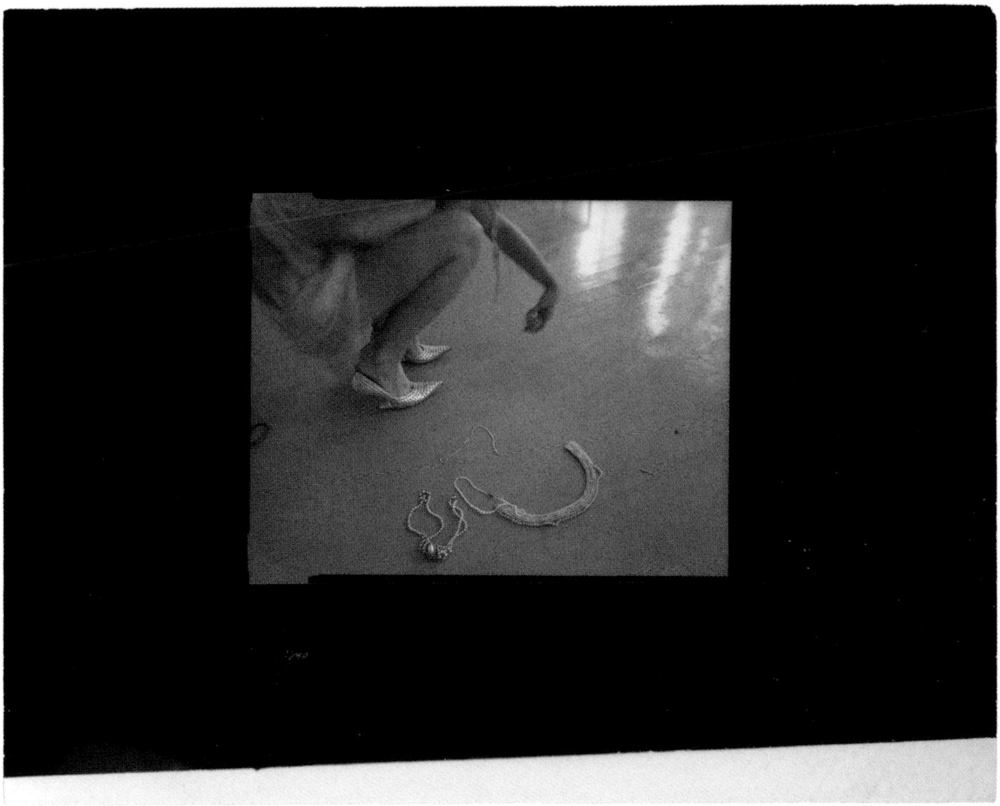

Untitled, New York, 1979–80

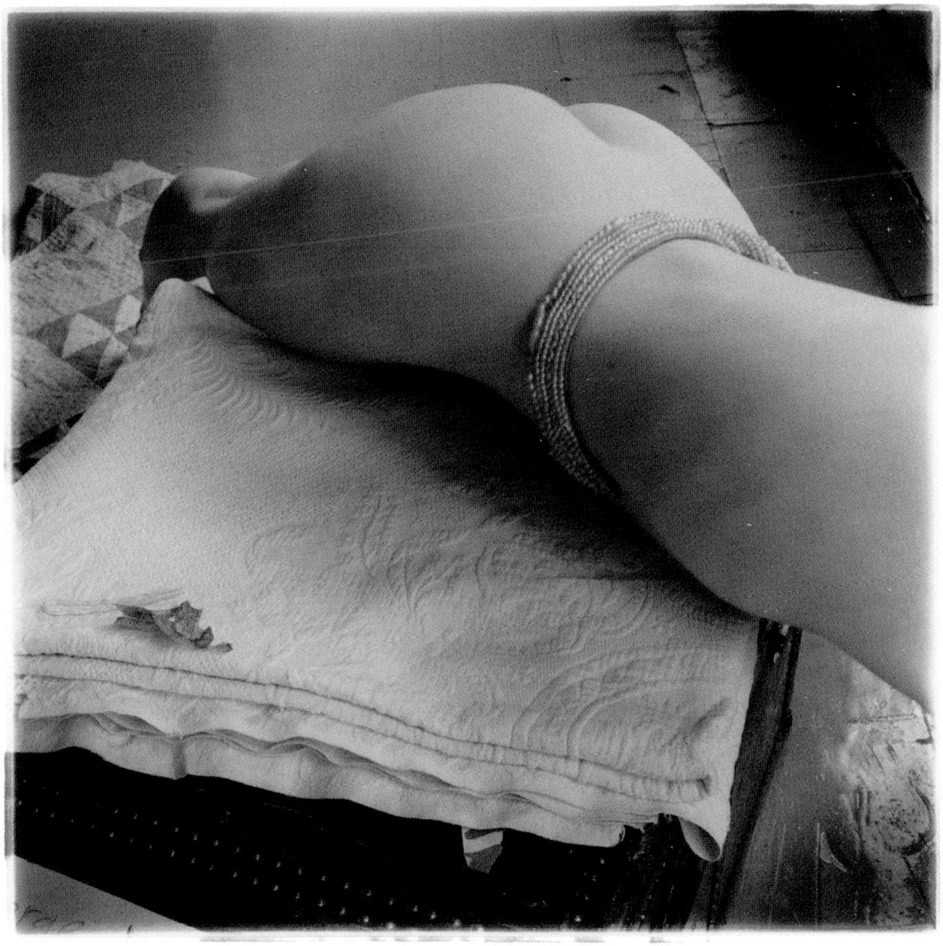

Untitled, New York, 1979–80

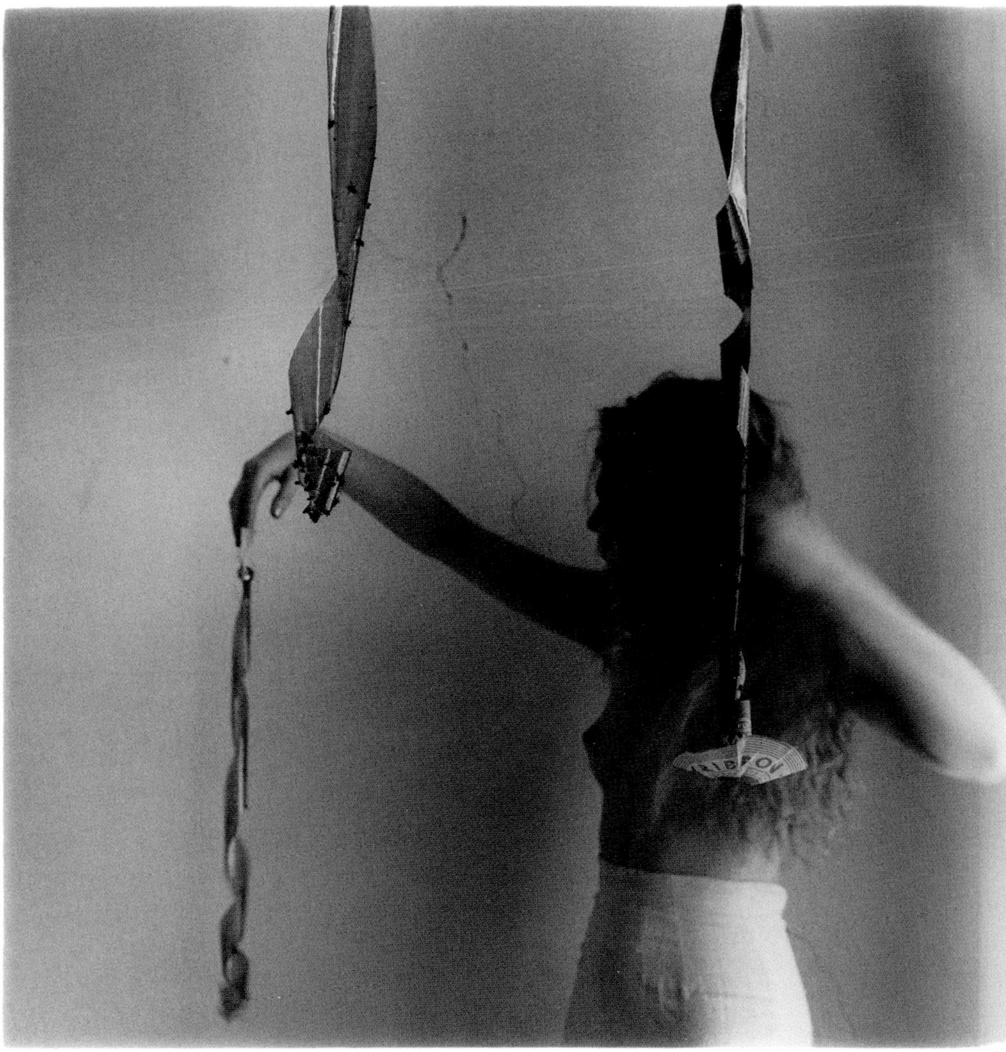

Untitled, New York, 1979–80

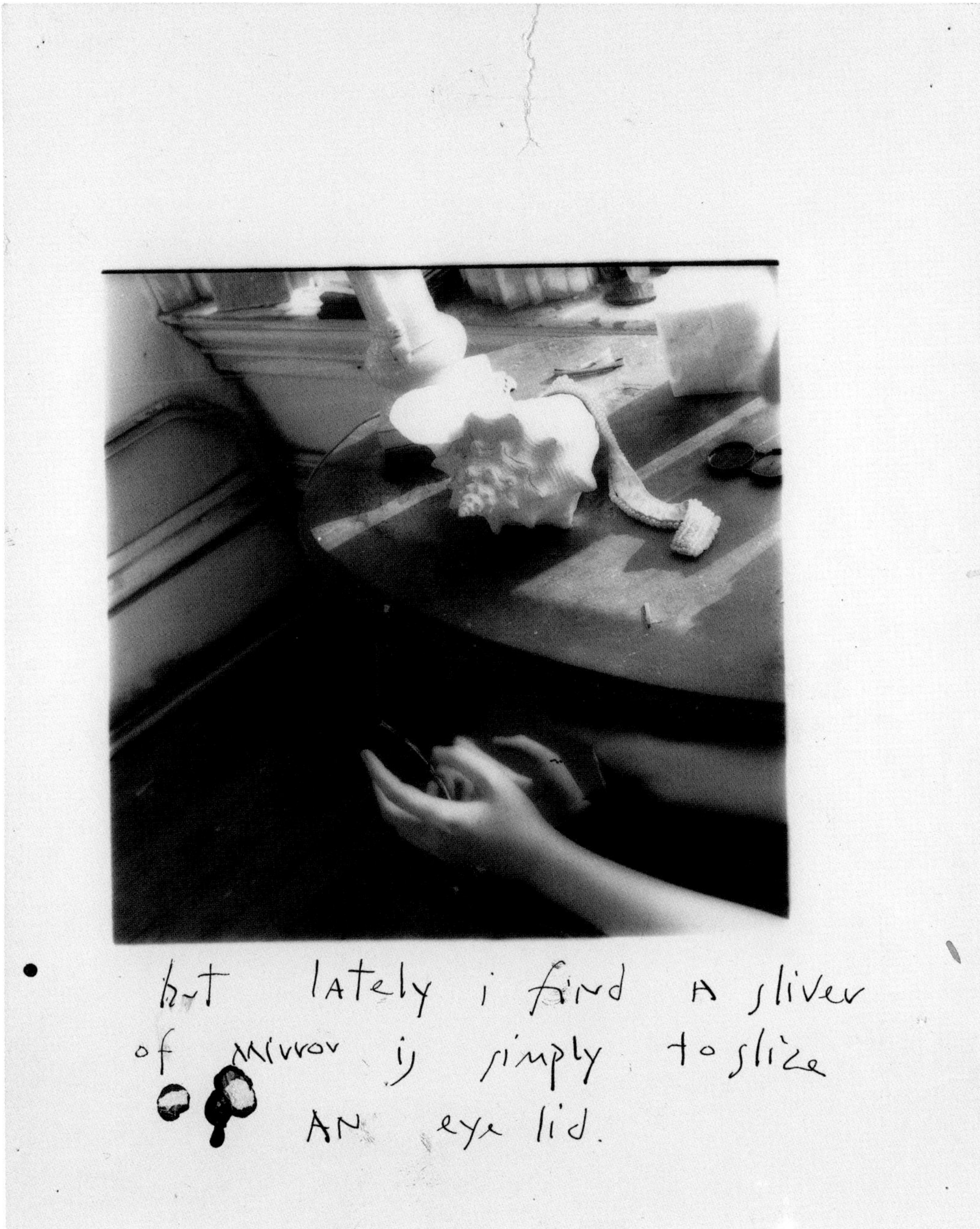

But lately I find a sliver of mirror is simply to slice an eyelid, New York, 1979–80

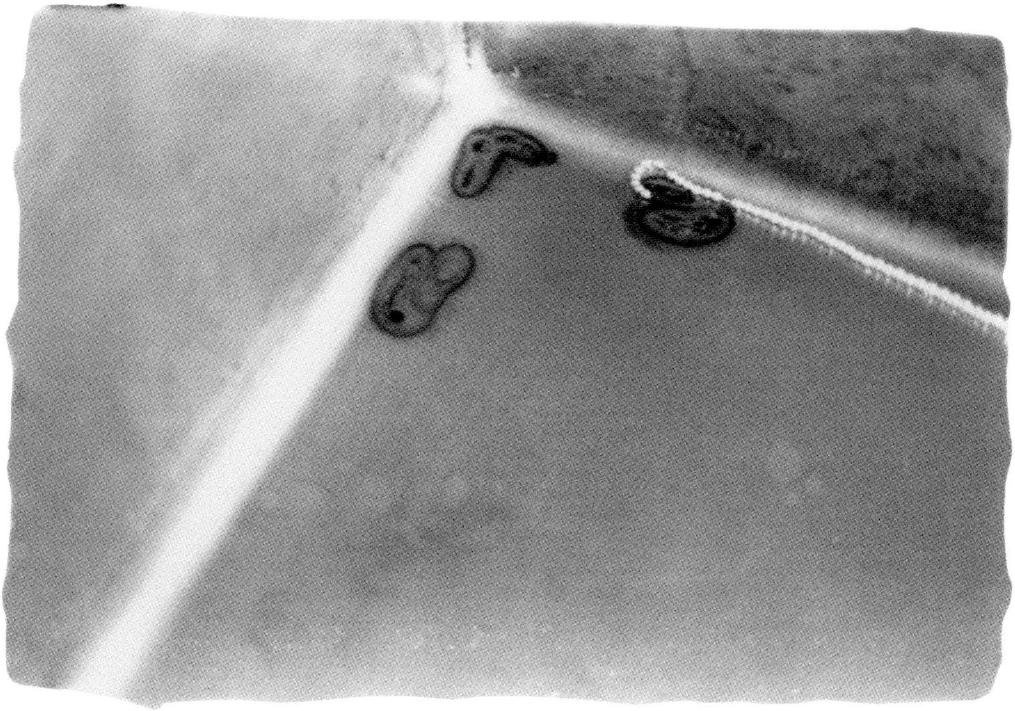

Untitled, New York, 1979–80

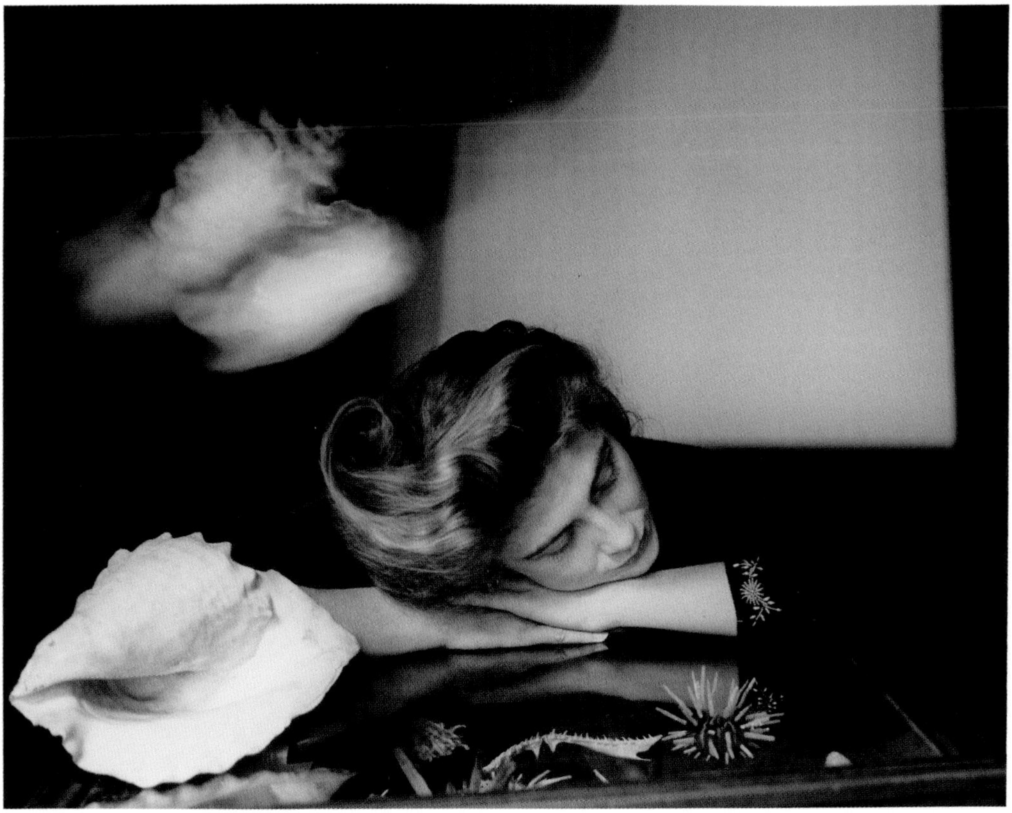

Untitled, New York, 1979–80

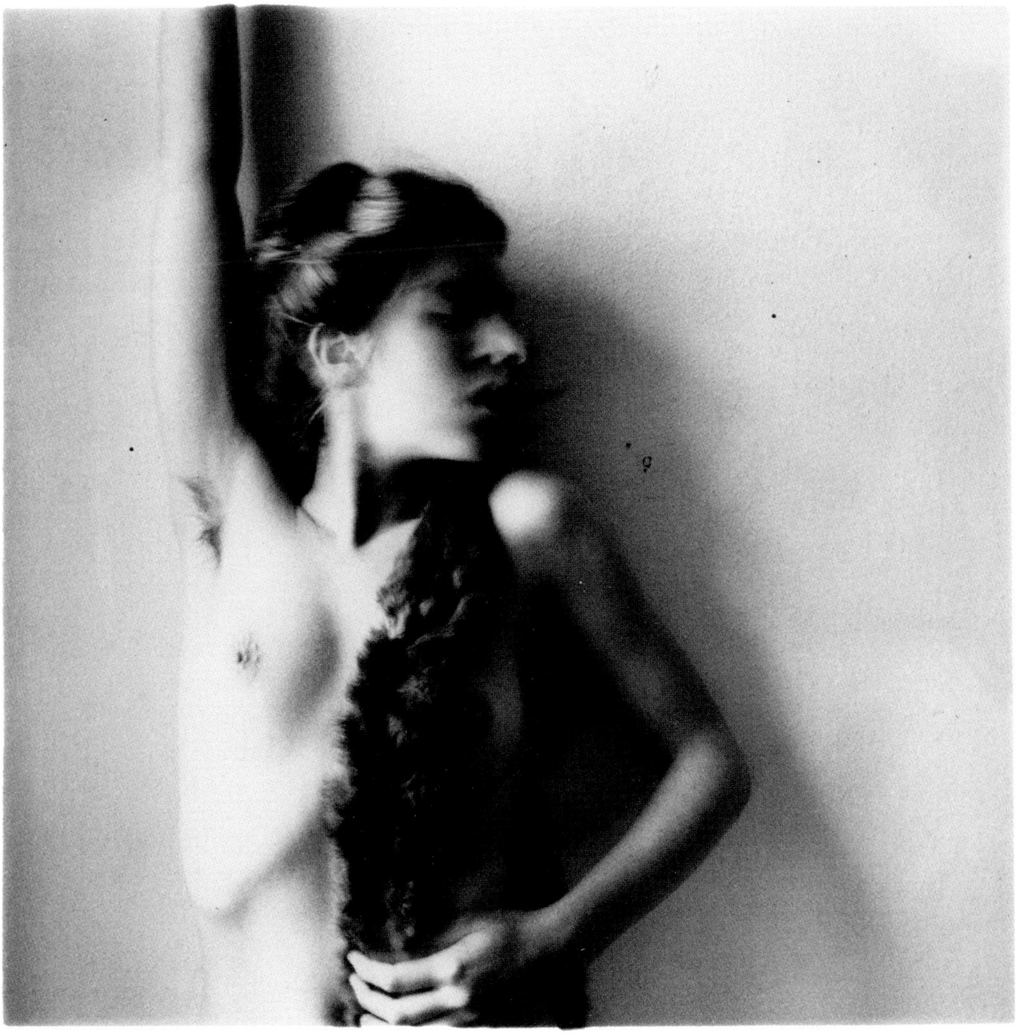

 Untitled, MacDowell Colony, Peterborough, New Hampshire, 1980

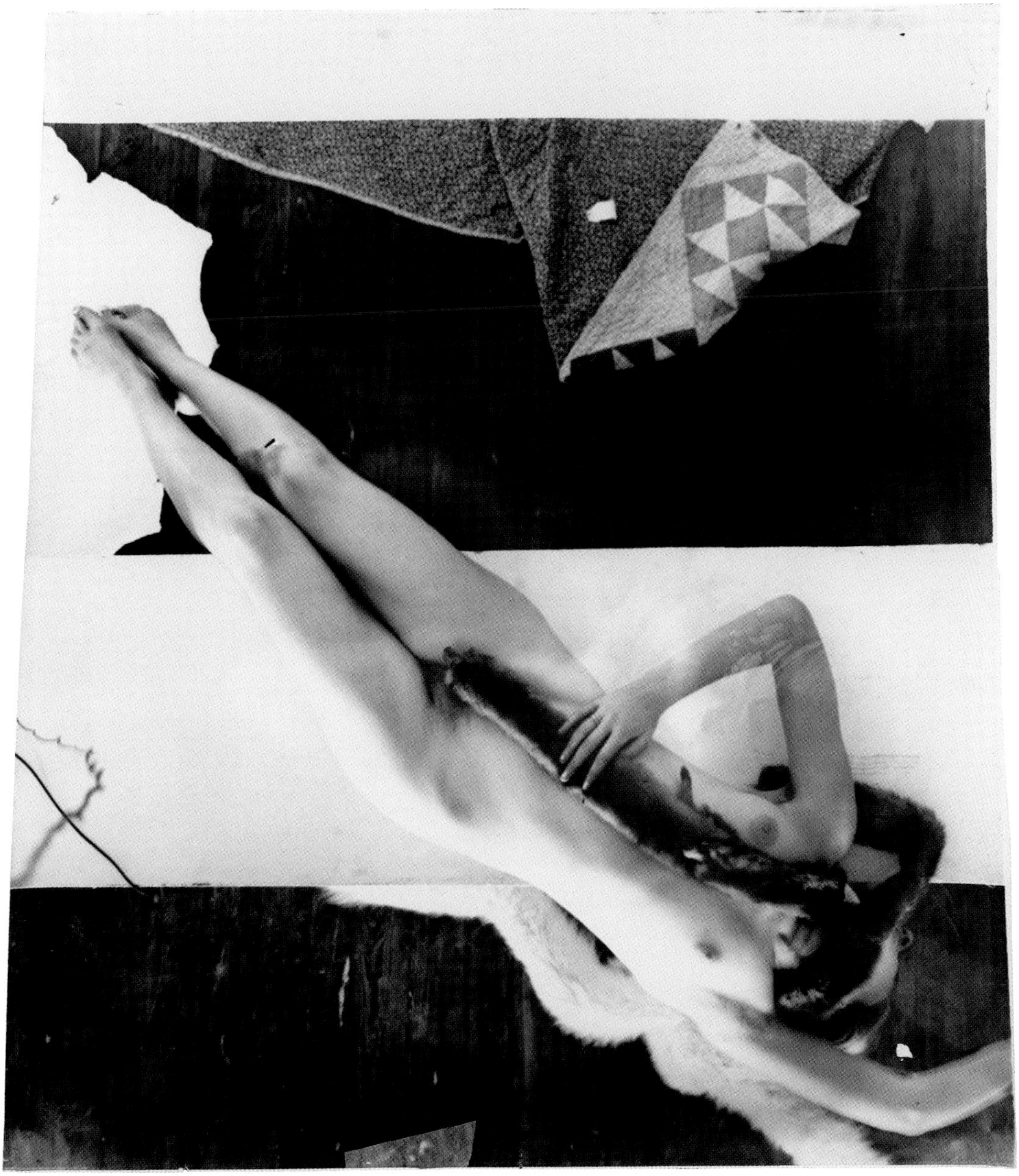

 Untitled (from Swan Song series), Providence, Rhode Island, 1978. 87 × 102.9 cm

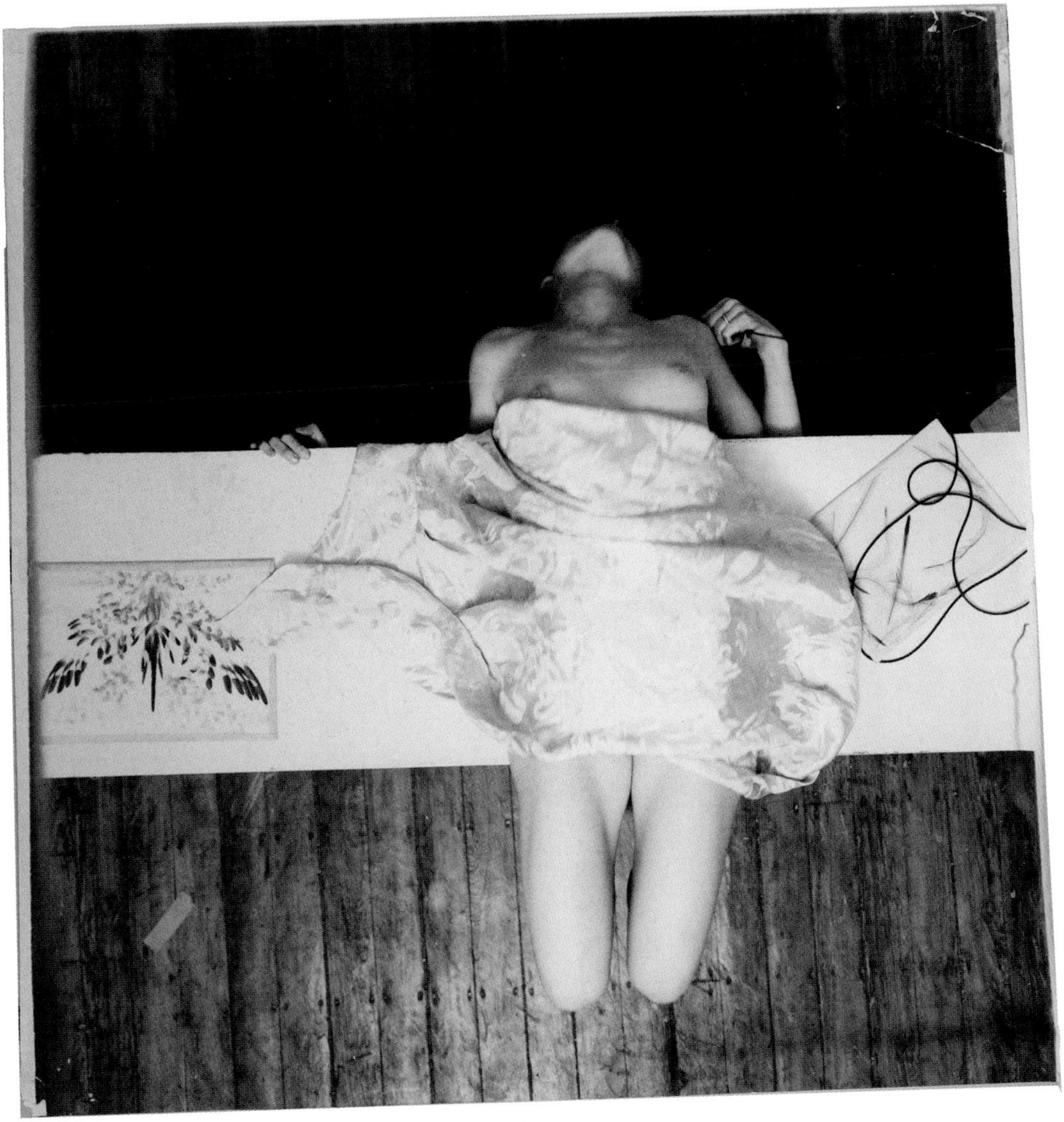

Untitled (from Swan Song series), Providence, Rhode Island, 1978. 99.7 × 94 cm

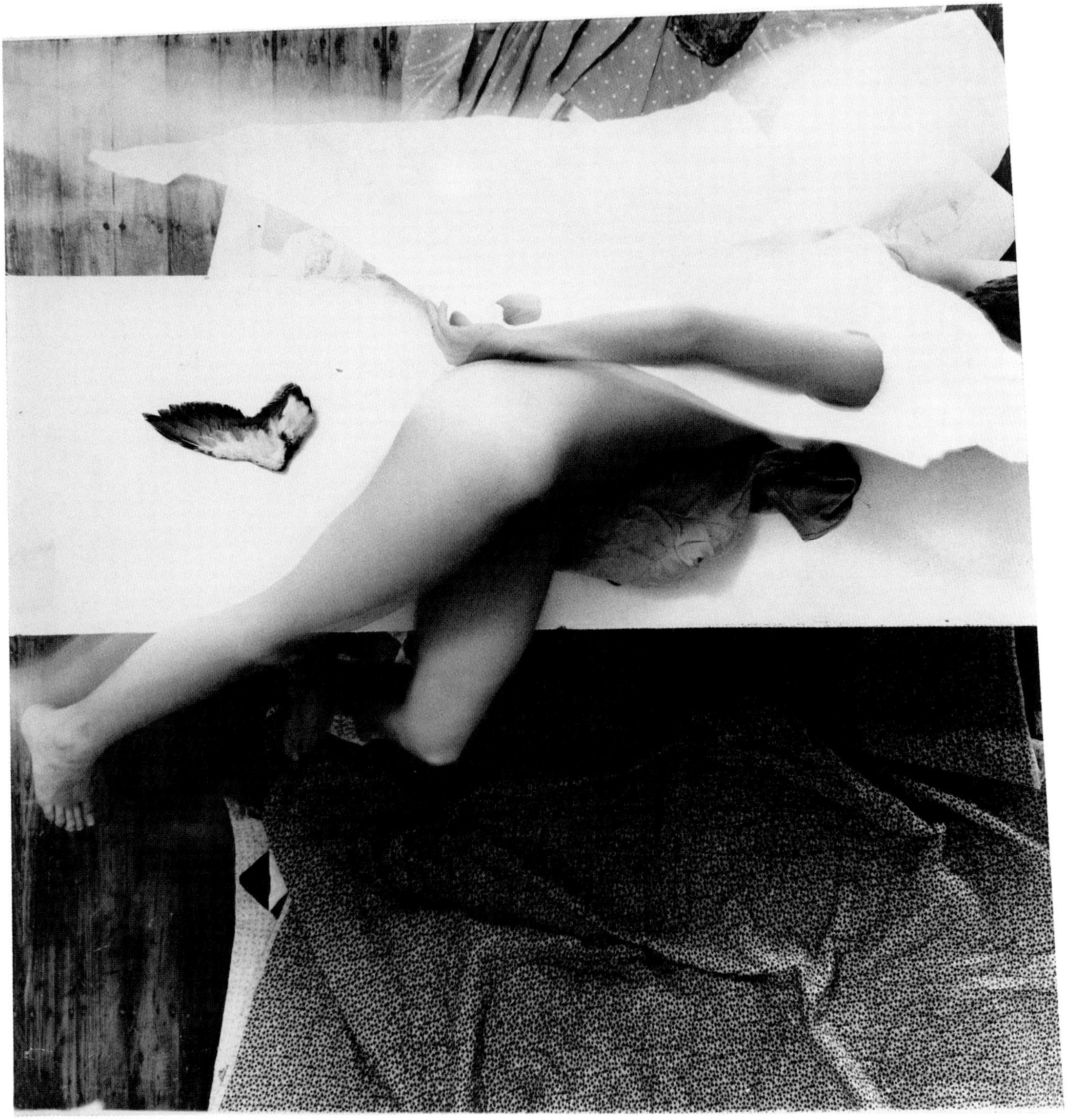

Untitled (from Swan Song series), Providence, Rhode Island, 1978. 89.5 × 83.8 cm

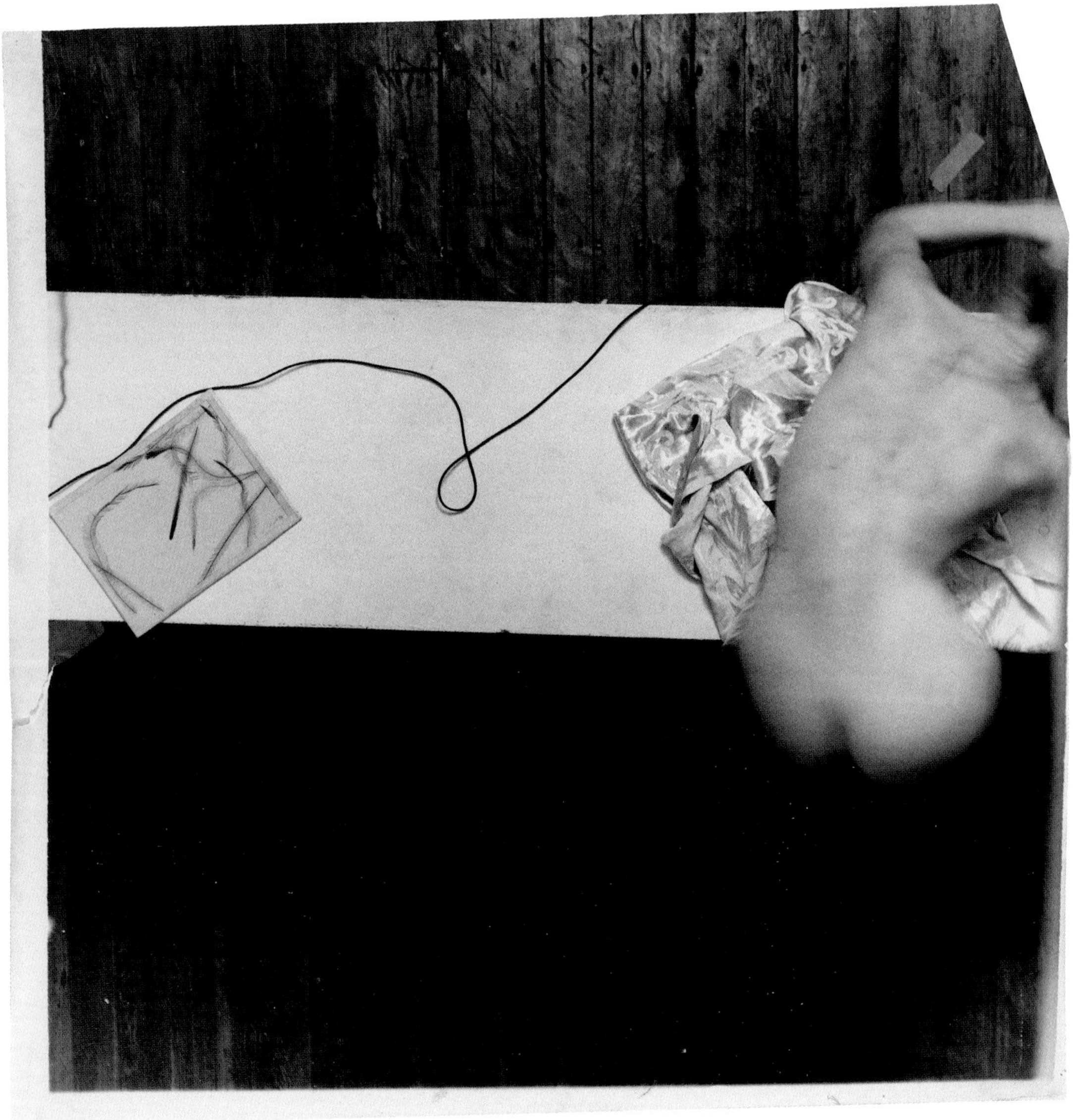

Untitled (from Swan Song series), Providence, Rhode Island, 1978. 94.6 × 97.2 cm

Caryatid (study for Temple Project), New York, 1980. 201 × 92 cm

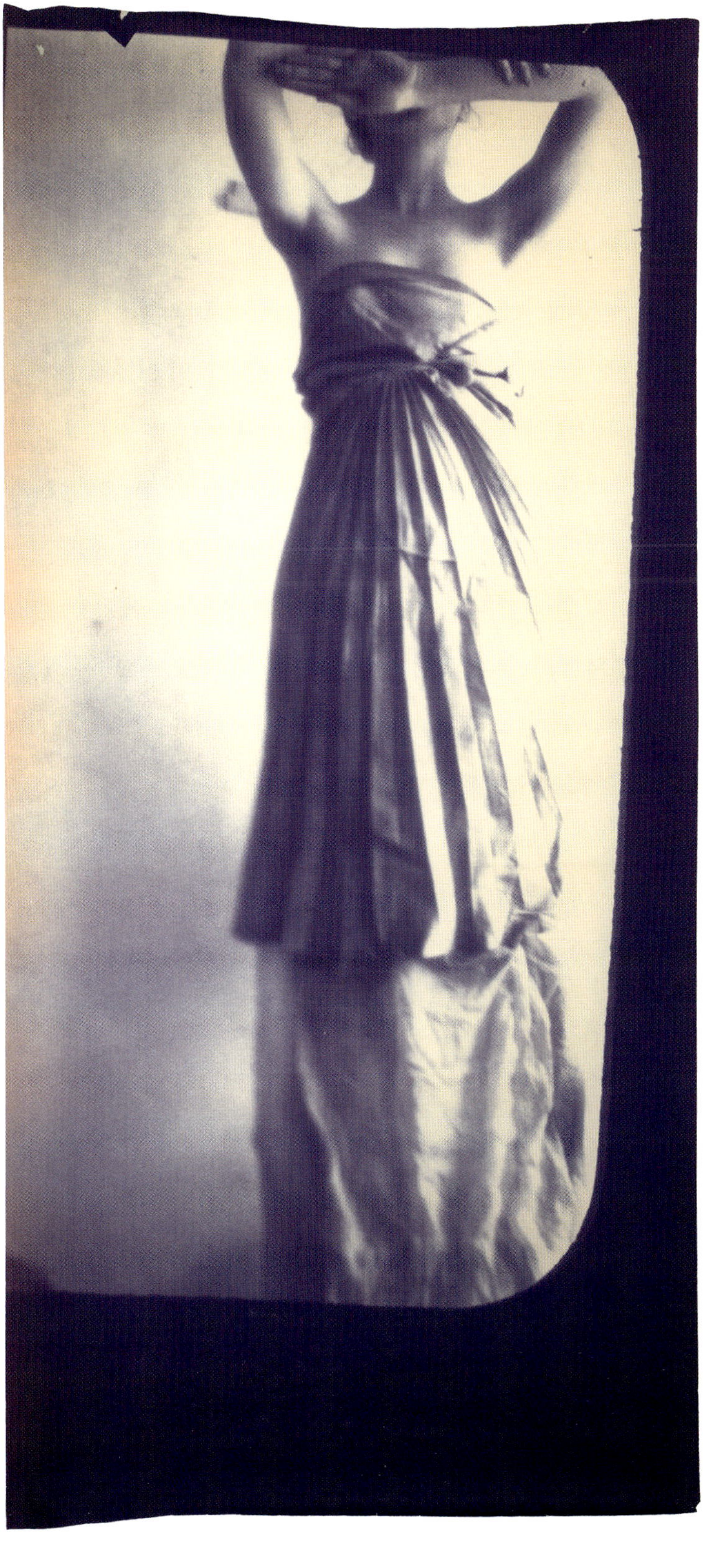

Caryatid, New York, 1980. 252.7 × 92 cm

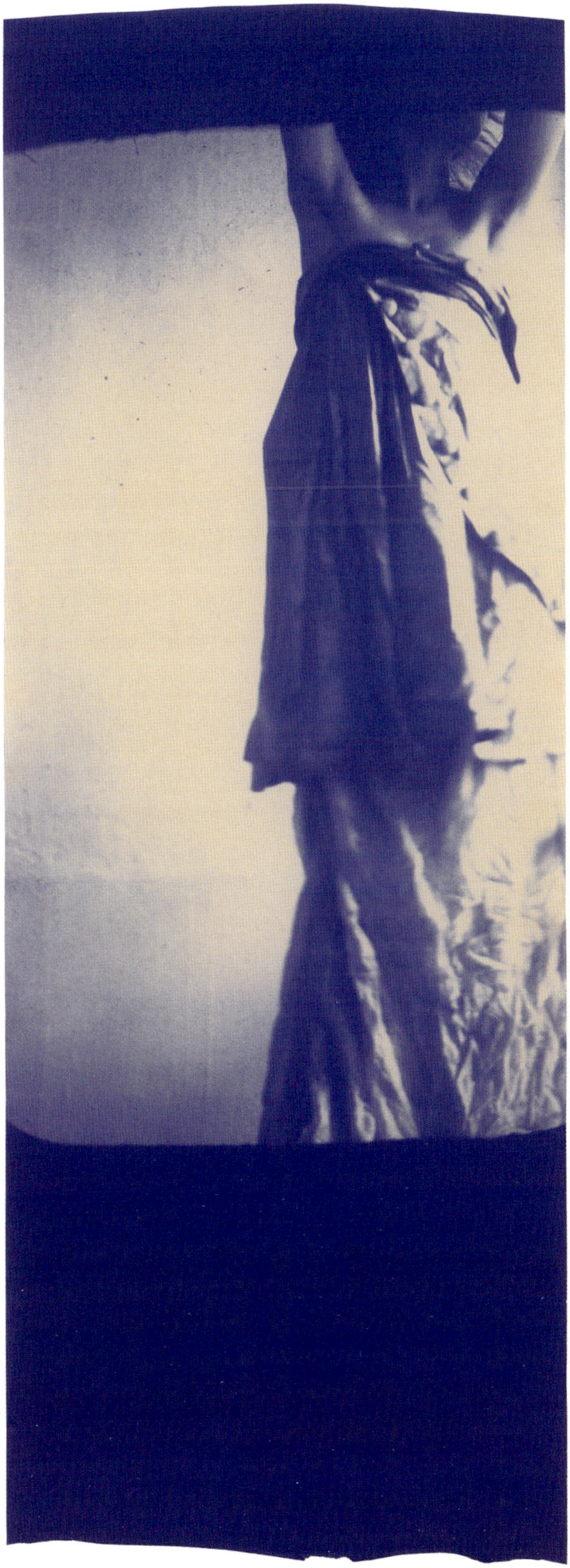

Caryatid, New York, 1980. 181 × 92 cm

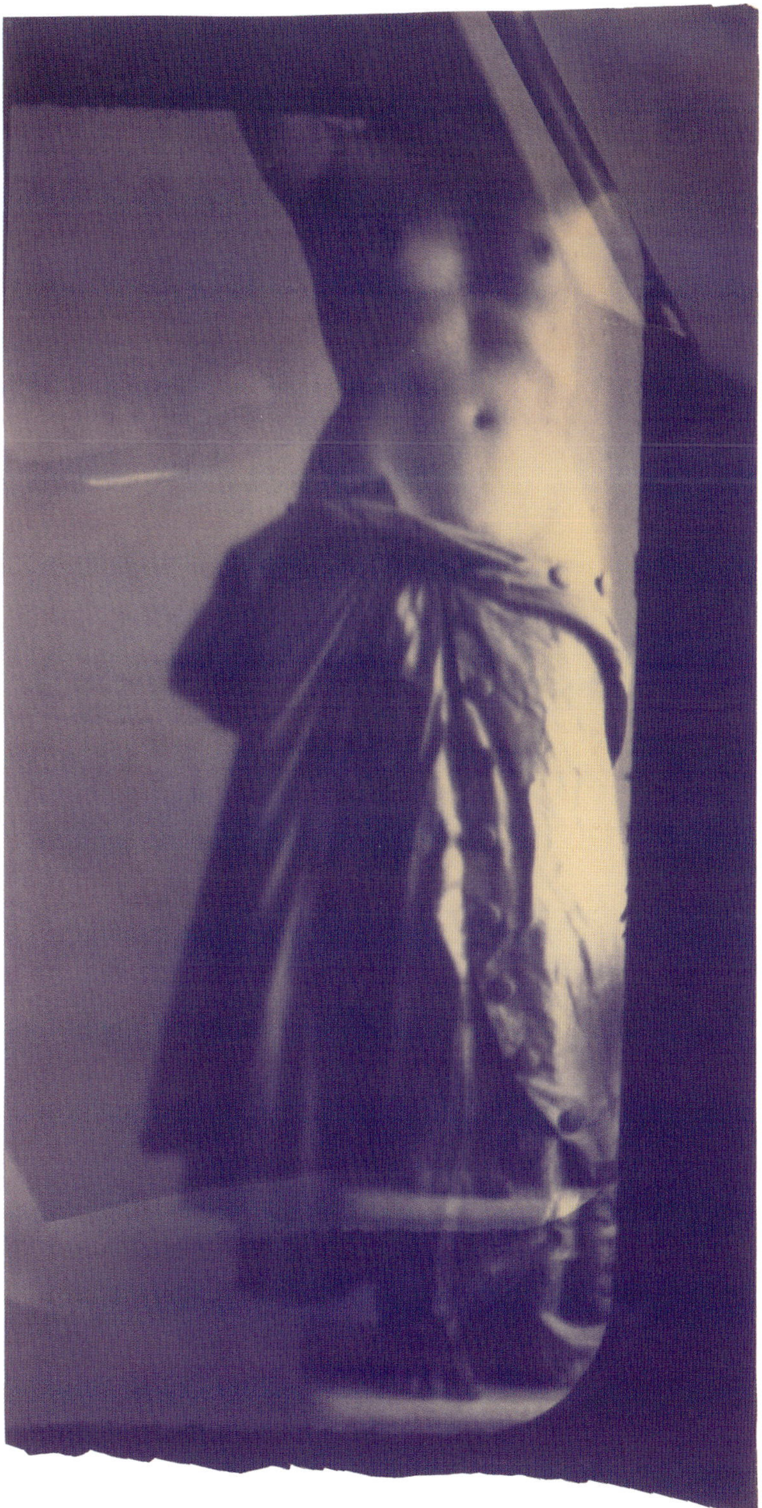

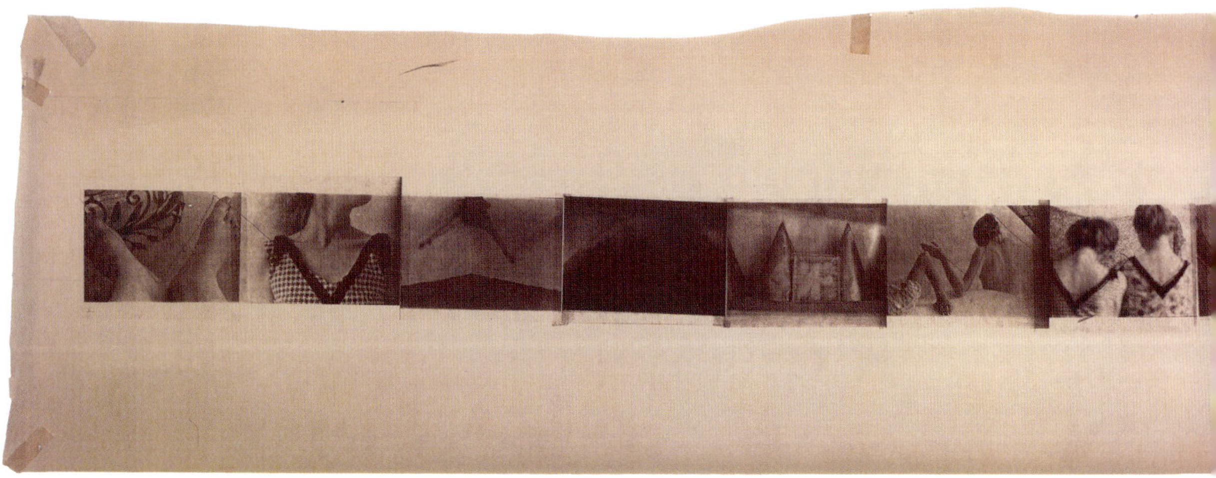

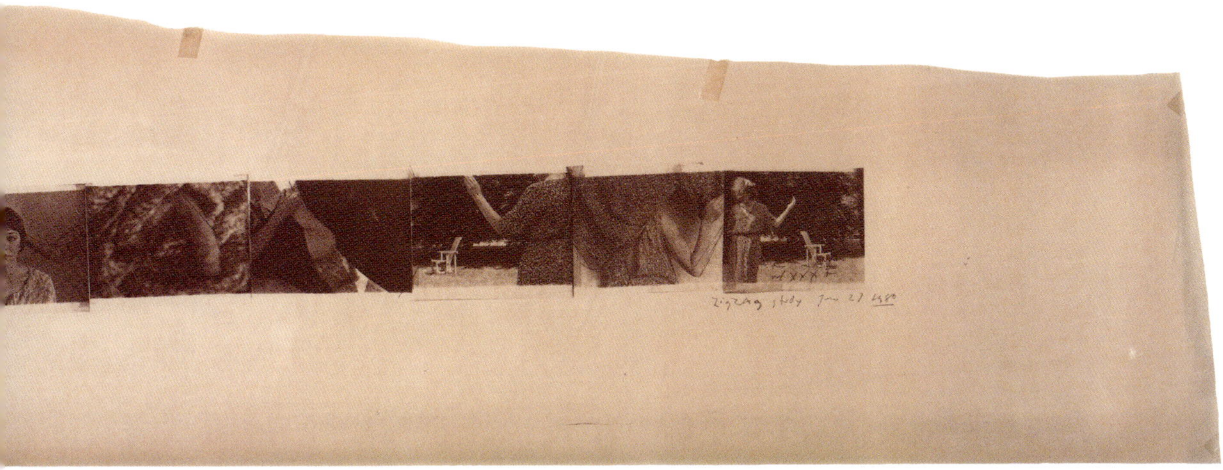

Zig Zag Study, New York, 1980. 36.2 × 191.8 cm

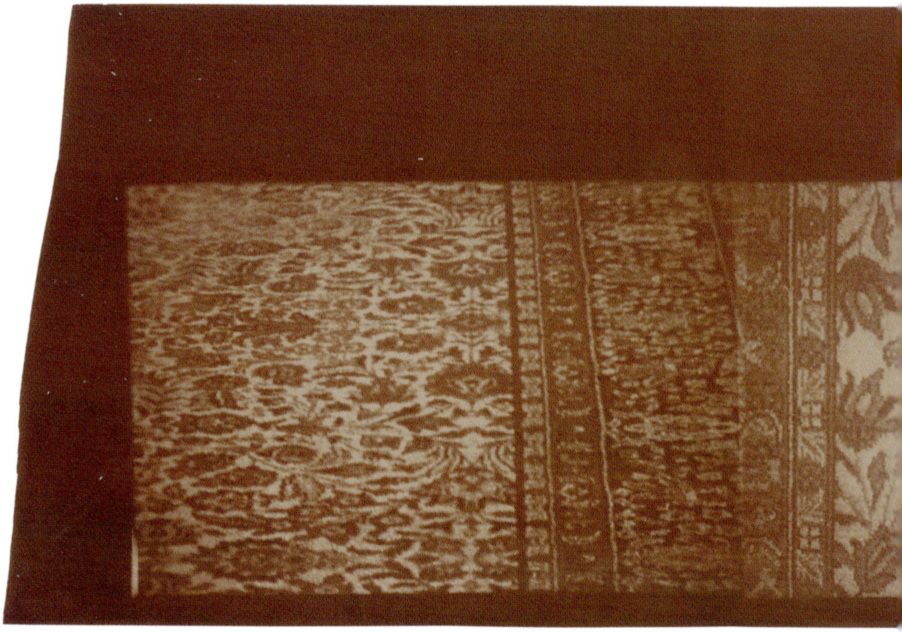

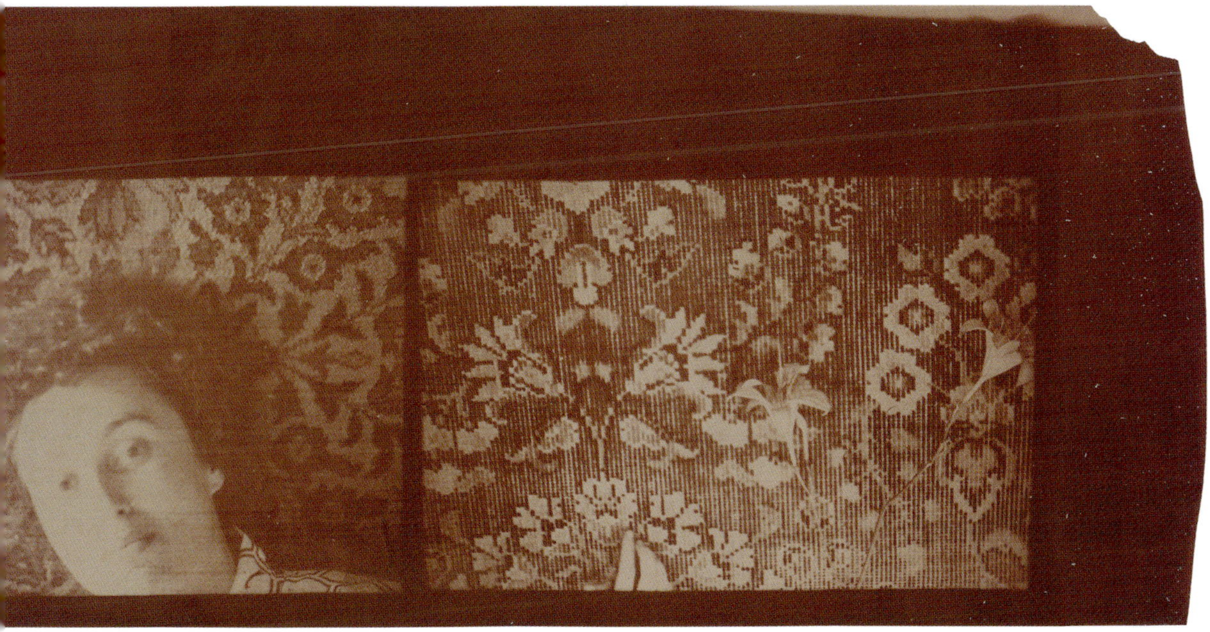

Head on Rug, New York, 1980. 92.7 × 317.5 cm

Out of the Grid, Into the Zigzag

GEORGE WOODMAN

The work of Francesca Woodman lies in the realm of still photography. Nevertheless, her images using the formal device of a zigzag are anything but still. They are restless pictures filled with motion. The viewer's glance is never permitted to halt and is urged onward to embrace sequences, consider episodes, submit to rhythms, and confront changes of identities. These images are less tied to the logic of "presentation," which is the core of still photography, and more the result of a choreography of images, an artful control of the irrepressible motion within them.

Growing up under Rocky Mountain skies, along with one brother, two cats, and piano lessons, Francesca lived in a lively family milieu of artists, which at the time meant she also grew up with The Grid. In the 1970s, modernist art – from Mondrian to Judd's sculptures and Johns's flags – was seen as formally based on the horizontal and vertical coordinates of The Grid. The critic Rosalind Krauss summed this up and criticized its weaknesses in a persuasive article published in *October* in the summer of 1979 entitled "Grids." This is the moment when Francesca deliberately adopted the zigzag, though one can see her attraction to it in many earlier photographs. She may not have read Krauss, but she was gifted with a precocious grasp of the historical moment in which she was an artist.

How did this happen?

The works in this exhibition show a freedom of structure that is a departure from the compositional strategies of her earlier photography. The zigzag in some instances is emphatically present as the primary motif, while in others it hovers as a possibility. Francesca not only liked its look, she also liked the word. She was liberated by words and their allure. As a reader and occasional imitator of Gertrude Stein, "zigzag" came easily to her lips.

Were there historical influences? Was she affected by Tintoretto, who rejected the Renaissance perspective box for the liberation of the free diagonal? We know that she visited friends in Venice, where she missed train connections and saw the paintings of Tintoretto. Was she influenced by them? Art history can happen while a girl licks an ice cream cone. How fortunate for the rest of us!

An audacious next step was the *Small sketch for a piece about bridges and tiaras,* 1980. Here the zigzag is transformed into a chain of looping and arching forms sailing across the paper. The imagery links together the bridge, among the highest achievements of "masculine" engineering, with the tiara, that accoutrement of "femininity" which bridges the brow of a queen. Her proposal includes a drawing of a sculpture of a tiaraed head and a collage depicting New York fantastically bridged and tiaraed. The proposal is modest in its realization, astonishing in its wealth of imagination.

This text was first published on the occasion of the exhibition *Francesca Woodman: Zigzag* at Victoria Miro Mayfair, London, 2014.

Biography

Francesca Woodman
Born in 1958 in Denver, Colorado
Died in 1981 in New York City

Solo Exhibitions

2015

I'm Trying My Hand at Fashion Photography, Marian Goodman Gallery, New York (exh. cat.)

2014

Francesca Woodman: Artist Rooms, Oriel Davies Gallery, Powys, Wales
Francesca Woodman: Zigzag, Victoria Miro Mayfair, London
Francesca Woodman: Artist Rooms, Bodelwyddan Castle, Denbighshire, Wales
Francesca Woodman: Works from the SAMMLUNG VERBUND, Vertical Gallery, Vienna (exh. cat.)

2012

Francesca Woodman, Mendes Wood, São Paulo
Francesca Woodman, Galeria Clara Maria Sels, Düsseldorf
Francesca Woodman: The Blueprints, Marian Goodman Gallery, New York (exh. cat.)

2011

Francesca Woodman, San Francisco Museum of Modern Art, San Francisco, California. Traveled to: Guggenheim Museum, New York (exh. cat.)
Francesca Woodman: Unseen Photographs and Selected Works, La Fábrica Galería, Madrid
Artist Rooms: Francesca Woodman, Ferens Art Gallery, Hull
Francesca Woodman Photographs 1977–1981, Il Museo del Louvre, Rome (exh. cat.)

2010

Francesca Woodman, Victoria Miro Gallery, London

2009

Francesca Woodman, La Fábrica Galería, Madrid
Francesca Woodman, Ingleby Gallery, Edinburgh
Artist Rooms: Francesca Woodman, Scottish National Gallery of Modern Art, Edinburgh
Francesca Woodman, Espacio AV, Murcia. Traveled to: SMS Contemporanea, Siena; Palazzo della Ragione, Milan (exh. cat.)

2008

Francesca Woodman, Galleria Carla Sozzani, Milan

2007

Francesca Woodman, Marian Goodman Gallery, New York
Francesca Woodman, Victoria Miro Gallery, London
Poetry and Dream Collection Display: Francesca Woodman, Tate Modern, London

2006

Francesca Woodman: Do I Still Exist If You Don't See Me?, Museum of New Art, Pontiac, Michigan
Antological/Retrospective Francesca Woodman, Biennale of Photography in Brescia, Galleria Massimo Minini, Brescia
Francesca Woodman, Galleria Il Capricorno, Venice
Francesca Woodman, George Woodman, Galerie Clara Maria Sels, Düsseldorf
Francesca Woodman, American Academy, Rome

2005

Francesca Woodman, Galerie Marian Goodman, Paris
Francesca Woodman, Galleria Davide Di Maggio, Berlin

2004

Francesca Woodman: Photographs 1975–1980, Marian Goodman Gallery, New York (exh. cat.)

2003

Francesca Woodman: Photographs, Herbert F. Johnson Museum of Art, Cornell University, Ithaca, New York (exh. cat.)
Francesca Woodman, Galerie Drantmann, Brussels
Francesca Woodman, Galerie Clara Marie Sels, Düsseldorf
Francesca Woodman, Kamel Mennour, Paris

2001

Francesca Woodman, Galerie Drantmann, Brussels

2000

Francesca Woodman: Providence, Roma, New York, Palazzo delle Esposizioni, Rome (exh. cat.)
Francesca Woodman, Victoria Miro Gallery, London

1999

Francesca Woodman, Marian Goodman Gallery, New York
Francesca Woodman, Bernard Toale Gallery, Boston, Massachusetts

1998

Francesca Woodman, Studio Guenzani, Milan

Francesca Woodman, Galleria Dryphoto, Prato

Francesca Woodman, Fondation Cartier pour l'art contemporain, Paris. Traveled to: Rencontres Internationales de la Photographie, Arles; Kunsthal, Rotterdam; Centro Cultural de Belém, Lisbon; The Photographers' Gallery, London; Centro Cultural TeclaSala, L'Hospitalet, Barcelona; Carla Sozzani Gallery, Milan; The Douglas Hyde Gallery, Dublin; PhotoEspana, Centro Cultural Conde Duque, Madrid (exh. cat.)

1996

Francesca Woodman, Galleria Civica, Modena (exh. cat.)

1995

Francesca Woodman, Casetti Galleria Libreria, Rome

1994

Francesca Woodman, PaceWildensteinMacGill, New York

1992

Francesca Woodman, Photographische Arbeiten/Photographic Works, Shedhalle, Zurich. Traveled to: Westfälischer Kunstverein, Münster; Kulturhuset, Stockholm; The Finnish Museum of Photography, Helsinki; DAAD Galerie, Berlin; Galleri F15, Alby, Moss (exh. cat.)

1989

Francesca Woodman: Photographic Work, Institute of Contemporary Art, Philadelphia, Pennsylvania

1986

Francesca Woodman: Photographic Work, Hunter College Art Gallery, New York. Traveled to: Wellesley College Museum, Wellesley, Massachusetts; University of Colorado Fine Arts Gallery, Boulder, Colorado; UCI Fine Arts Gallery, University of California, Irvine, California; Krannert Art Museum, Champaign, Illinois (exh. cat.)

1978

Swan Song, Woods-Gerry Gallery, Rhode Island School of Design, Providence, Rhode Island

Francesca Woodman, Libreria Maldoror, Rome

1976

Francesca Woodman, Addison Gallery of American Art, Andover, Massachusetts

Group Exhibitions

2015

Francesca Woodman & Birgit Jürgenssen. Works from the collection SAMMLUNG VERBUND, Merano Arte, Bolzano
America Is Hard to See, Whitney Museum of American Art, New York
Bare Wunder, Sies + Höke, Düsseldorf
Edith Schloss: Still Life, Myths and Mountains, A Retrospective, Sundaram Tagore Gallery, New York
The Self: Portraits of the Artists in Their Absence, The National Academy Museum, New York
Absence, David Risley Gallery, Copenhagen
Pliure (Prologue–La part du feu), Fondation Calouste Gulbenkian, Paris (exh. cat.)
Sleepless: The Bed in History and Contemporary Art, 21er Haus, Vienna (exh. cat.)

2014

Secret Passions, Private Flemish Collections, Lille3000, Euralille (exh. cat.)
Sigmund Freud and the Play on the Burden of Representation, 21er Haus, Vienna
Made by... Feito Por Brasileiros, Cidade Matarazzo, São Paulo
Self-Timer Stories, Austrian Cultural Forum, New York. Traveled to: Museum der Moderne, Salzburg; MUSAC Museo de Arte Contemporáneo de Castilla y León, León (exh. cat.)
WOMAN: *The Feminist Avant-Garde from the 1970s, Works from the SAMMLUNG VERBUND*, *Vienna,* BOZAR, Palais des Beaux-Arts, Brussels. Traveled to: Mjellby Konstmuseum, Halmstad; Hamburger Kunsthalle, Hamburg (exh. cat.)

2013

Biographical Forms: Construction and Individual Mythology, Museo Nacional Centro de Arte Reina Sofía, Madrid (exh. cat.)
Shaping a Modern Identity: Portraits from the Joseph and Charlotte Lichtenberg Collection, The Phillips Collection, Washington, DC
Reproductibilitat 1.0, Es Baluard Museu d'Art Modern i Contemporani de Palma, Palma, Illes Balears
Memorias de la obsolescencia: Selección de Videos en la Colección Ella Fontanals-Cisneros, Centro de Arte Contemporáneo Wifredo Lam, Havana
L'altro ritratto, MART Museo d'Arte Moderna e Contemporanea di Trento e Rovereto, Rovereto, Trento (exh. cat.)
Between Memory and Archive, Museu Coleção Berardo, Lisbon
Homebodies, Museum of Contemporary Art Chicago, Chicago, Illinois
Altérité: Je est un autre, Espace Cultural Louis Vuitton, Paris
I, You, We, Whitney Museum of American Art, New York
(Un)seen, Fountain Gallery, New York
The Four Woodmans, Nina Freudenheim Gallery, Buffalo, New York

2012

The Angels of Klee, Zentrum Paul Klee, Bern. Traveled to: Museum Folkwang, Essen; Hamburger Kunsthalle, Hamburg (exh. cat.)

The Serial Portrait: Photography and Identity in the Last One Hundred Years, National Gallery of Art, Washington, DC

Letizia Battaglia/Francesca Woodman, Galleria Massimo Minini, Brescia

"Mindscapes" or how to make the invisible visible?, La Centrale Électrique, Brussels

Wavelengths, Toronto International Film Festival, Toronto

Pink Caviar, Louisiana Museum of Modern Art, Humlebæk (exh. cat.)

The Woodmans, Gallery Diet, Miami, Florida

Spies in the House of Art: Photography, Film and Video, Metropolitan Museum of Art, New York

In Wonderland: The Surrealist Adventures of Women Artists in Mexico and the United States, Los Angeles County Museum of Art, Los Angeles, California. Traveled to: Musée national des beaux-arts du Québec; Museo de Arte Moderno, Mexico City

2011

Alice in Wonderland, Tate, Liverpool. Traveled to: Museo di Arte Contemporanea di Trento e Rovereto, Rovereto; Hamburger Kunsthalle, Hamburg

Nothing in the World but Youth, Turner Contemporary, Margate, Kent

Off the Wall, Museu de Arte Contemporânea de Serralves, Porto

2010

Betty, Charlie, Francesca & George, Samson Projects, Boston, Massachusetts

Brune/Blonde, La Cinémathèque française–Musée du Cinéma, Paris

Incognito: The Hidden Self-Portrait, Yancey Richardson Gallery, New York

The Surreal House, Barbican Art Gallery, London (exh. cat.)

Donna: Avanguardia Femminista Negli Anni '70 dalla SAMMLUNG VERBUND di Vienna, Galleria nazionale d'arte moderna e contemporanea, Rome (exh. cat.)

2009

Angels of Anarchy: Women Artists and Surrealism, Manchester Art Gallery, Manchester (exh. cat.)

Camuflajes, La Casa Encendida, Madrid. Traveled to: Espacio para el Arte Caja Madrid, Zaragoza; Museo del Patrimonio Municipal, Ayuntamiento de Málaga, Málaga; Espai Cultural Caja Madrid, Barcelona (exh. cat.)

Fail Again Fail Better 2, MK Galerie, Berlin

Transitory Objects, Thyssen-Bornemisza Contemporary Art, Vienna (exh. cat.)

The Female Gaze: Women Look at Women, Cheim & Read, New York

Subversive Spaces: Contemporary Art and Surrealism, Whitworth Art Gallery, University of Manchester, Manchester. Traveled to: Compton Verney, Warwickshire; Sainsbury Center for Visual Arts, University of East Anglia, Norwich

This Is Not a Fashion Photograph: Selections from the ICP Collection, International Center of Photography, New York

2008

Diana and Actaion–The Forbidden Sight of Nudity, Museum Kunstpalast, Düsseldorf (exh. cat.)

Conversations, Kettle's Yard, University of Cambridge, Cambridge

Darkside–Part One: Photographic Desire and Sexuality Photographed, Fotomuseum Winterthur, Winterthur (exh. cat.)

Implant, Horticultural Society of New York, UBS Art Gallery, New York

Female Trouble, Pinakothek der Moderne, Munich (exh. cat.)

Freeway Balconies, Deutsche Guggenheim, Berlin (exh. cat.)

2007

Autoritratto/Autobiografia, Museo Hendrik Christian Andersen, Galleria Nazionale d'Arte Moderna, Rome (exh. cat.)

The Woodman Family, Biagiotti Progetto Arte, Florence (exh. cat.)

30/40, A Selection: Forty Artists from Thirty Years of Exhibitions at Marian Goodman Gallery (Part II), Marian Goodman Gallery, New York (exh. cat.)

Ellipsis: Chantal Akerman, Lili Dujourie, Francesca Woodman, Museo Tamayo Arte Contemporáneo, Mexico City. Traveled to: Lunds konsthall, Lund; Dundee Contemporary Arts, Dundee (exh. cat.)

Francesca Woodman & Richard Serra, Ingleby Gallery, Edinburgh

Held Together with Water: Art from the SAMMLUNG VERBUND, MAK, Vienna. Traveled to: Istanbul Museum of Modern Art, Istanbul (exh. cat.)

WACK! Art and the Feminist Revolution, The Geffen Contemporary at MOCA, Los Angeles, California. Traveled to: National Museum of Women in the Arts, Washington, DC; MoMA PS1, Long Island City, New York; Vancouver Art Gallery, Vancouver (exh. cat.)

Exposed: Defining Moments in Photography from the MCA Collection, Museum of Contemporary Art, Chicago, Illinois

D'Ombra, Museo d'Arte Provincia di Nuoro, Nuoro

2006

Photography and the Self: The Legacy of F. Holland Day, Whitney Museum of American Art, New York

D'Ombra, Palazzo delle Papesse, Siena (exh. cat.)

GORGE(l): Oppression and Relief in Art, Royal Museum of Fine Arts, Antwerp (exh. cat.)

Biennale Internazionale di Fotografia di Brescia, Museo di Santa Giulia, Brescia

4th Berlin Biennial for Contemporary Art, KW Institute of Contemporary Art, Berlin (exh. cat.)

Masquerade: Representation and the Self in Contemporary Art, Museum of Contemporary Art, Sydney (exh. cat.)

Dormir, rêver… et autres nuits, CAPC musée d'art contemporain de Bordeaux, Bordeaux (exh. cat.)

Francesca Woodman & George Woodman, Galerie Clara Maria Sels, Düsseldorf

Screened and Selected: Recent Photography, Film, and Video Acquisitions, 1999–2000, Middlebury College Museum of Art, Middlebury, Vermont (exh. cat.)

2005

Indeterminate States: Video in the Ella Fontanals-Cisneros Collection, CIFO, Miami, Florida (exh. cat.)

Taking Place: Photographs from the Prentice and Paul Sack Collection, San Francisco Museum of Modern Art, San Francisco, California (exh. cat.)

Video Works Charles Woodman: Photographs Francesca Woodman, Shirley/Jones Gallery, Yellow Springs, Ohio

Die Regierung: Paradiesische Handlungsräume, Secession, Association of Visual Artists, Vienna

Photography and Fashion, Megaron, Athens Concert Hall, Athens (exh. cat.)

Profumo di Donna, Galleria del Tasso, Bergamo (exh. cat.)

2004

How do we want to be governed?, MACBA–Museu d'Art Contemporani de Barcelona, Barcelona. Traveled to: Miami Art Central, Miami, Florida; Witte de With Center for Contemporary Art, Rotterdam (exh. cat.)

Reflecting the Mirror, Marian Goodman Gallery, New York

That bodies speak has been known for a long time, Generali Foundation, Vienna (exh. cat.)

Ideal and Reality: A History of the Nude, Galleria d'Arte Moderna, Bologna

2003

The Disembodied Spirit, Bowdoin College Museum of Art, Brunswick, Maine. Traveled to: Kemper Museum of Contemporary Art, Kansas City, Missouri; Austin Museum of Art, Austin, Texas (exh. cat.)

Incommunicado, Sainsbury Centre for Visual Arts, Norwich. Traveled to: City Art Centre, Edinburgh; Cornerhouse, Manchester (exh. cat.)

After Image, The Fruitmarket Gallery, Edinburgh. Traveled to: Helsinki City Art Museum, Helsinki; Victoria Miro Gallery, London

Claude Cahun, Francesca Woodman, and Justine Kurland, Susanne Hilberry Gallery, Ferndale, Michigan

2002

Hexenwahn, Deutsches Historisches Museum, Berlin

2001

Camera Women, Princeton University Art Museum, Princeton, New Jersey. Traveled to: The Frances Lehman Loeb Art Center, Vassar College, Poughkeepsie, New York (exh. cat.)

Relative Positions, Contemporary Arts Museum, Houston, Texas (exh. cat.)

The Big Id, James Cohan Gallery, New York

2000

The Wounded Diva: Hysteria, Body, Technology in 20thCentury Art, Galerie im Taxispalais, Innsbruck. Traveled to: Städtische Galerie im Lenbachhaus, Munich; Staatliche Kunsthalle, Baden-Baden (exh. cat.)
Raw, Victoria Miro Gallery, London

1999

The American Century: Art & Culture, 1950–2000, The Whitney Museum of American Art, New York (exh. cat.)
Galerie Lelong, New York

1998

Space/Sight/Self, David and Alfred Smart Museum of Art, University of Chicago, Chicago, Illinois (exh. cat.)
F-Comme Photographie, Fri Art–Centre d'art contemporain–Kunsthalle Freiburg, Fribourg
The Skopelos Center, Skopelos
From the Heart: The Power of Photography–A Collector's Choice, The Sondra Gilman Collection, South Texas Institute of the Arts, Corpus Christi, Texas (exh. cat.)
Mirror Images: Women, Surrealism and Self-Representations, MIT, List Visual Arts Center, Cambridge. Traveled to: Miami Art Museum, Miami, Florida; San Francisco Museum of Modern Art, San Francisco, California (exh. cat.)

1997

Recent Acquisitions, MoMA–Museum of Modern Art, New York
Objectif corps, The Montreal Museum of Fine Arts, Montreal
Amours, Fondation Cartier pour l'art contemporain, Paris (exh. cat.)
Im Reich der Phantome, Museum Abteiberg, Monchengladbach. Traveled to: Kunsthalle Krems, Krems; Fotomuseum Winterthur, Winterthur (exh. cat.)
Engel, Engel, Kunsthalle Wien, Vienna. Traveled to: Galerie Rudolfinum, Prague (exh. cat.)

1994

Inside the Visible: Begin the Beguine in Flanders, Kanaal Art Foundation, Kortrijk. Traveled to: Institute of Contemporary Art, Boston, Massachusetts; National Museum of Women in the Arts, Washington, DC; Whitechapel Gallery, London (exh. cat.)

1992

Current 92: The Absent Body, Institute of Contemporary Art, Boston, Massachusetts
Sprung in die Zeit, Museum für Moderne Kunst, Photographie und Architektur, Berlin (exh. cat.)

1989

Vanishing Presence, Walker Art Center, Minneapolis, Minnesota. Traveled to: The Detroit Institute of Art, Detroit, Michigan; Winnipeg Art Center, Winnipeg; High Museum of Art, Atlanta, Georgia; Herbert F. Johnson Museum of Art, Cornell University, Ithaca; Virginia Museum of Fine Arts, Richmond, Virginia (exh. cat.)

1988

Identity: Representation of the Self, Whitney Museum of American Art, Downtown at Federal Reserve Plaza, New York

Sexual Difference: Both Sides of the Camera, Wallach Art Gallery, Columbia University, New York (exh. cat.)

1985

Memento Mori, Goldie Paley Gallery, Moore College of Art and Design, Philadelphia, Pennsylvania. Traveled to: Centro Cultural de Arte Contemporáneo, Mexico City (exh. cat.)

1980

Pictorialism, Daniel Wolf, Inc., New York

Beyond Photography 80, The Alternative Museum, New York (exh. cat.)

Friends of the Gallery, Daniel Wolf, Inc., New York

1978

Group Show, Rhode Island School of Design Gallery in Palazzo Cenci, Rome

Cinque Giovani Artisti, Galleria Ugo Ferranti, Rome

1977

Juried Competition, Woods-Gerry Gallery, Rhode Island School of Design, Providence, Rhode Island

Photographs and Portraiture, Womanspace, Boulder, Colorado

1976

Juried Competition, Woods-Gerry Gallery, Rhode Island School of Design, Providence, Rhode Island

Selected Bibliography

Francesca Woodman. I'm Trying My Hand at Fashion Photography, text by Alison M. Gingeras. New York: Marian Goodman Gallery, 2015.

Francesca Woodman. Works from the Sammlung Verbund, ed. Gabriele Schor and Elisabeth Bronfen, texts by Betsy Berne, Johannes Binotto, Elisabeth Bronfen, Gabriele Schor, Abigail Solomon-Godeau, and Beate Söntgen, Verlag der Buchhandlung Walter König, Cologne. New York: D.A.P. Distributed Art Publishers, Inc., 2014.

Isabella Pedicini, *Francesca Woodman. The Roman years: between flesh and film*, introduction by Gerry Badger. Rome: Contrasto, 2012.

Francesca Woodman, ed. Corey Keller, texts by Jennifer Blessing, Julia Bryan-Wilson, and Corey Keller, San Francisco Museum of Modern Art, San Francisco. New York: D.A.P. Distributed Art Publishers, Inc., 2011.

Francesca Woodman : Roma 1977–1981, ed. Giuseppe Casetti and Francesco Stocchi, texts by Giuseppe (Cristiano) Casetti, Edith Schloss, and Francesca Woodman, Il Museo del Louvre. Rome: AGMA Publishing, 2011.

Francesca Woodman, ed. Marco Pierini, texts by Rossella Caruso, Lorenzo Fusi, Marco Pierini, and Isabel Tejeda, Palazzo della Ragione. Milan: Silvana Editoriale Spa, 2010.

Francesca Woodman Retrospectiva, ed. Isabel Tejeda, texts by Mieke Bal, Fernando Castro Flórez, Rosalind Krauss, and Marco Pierini, Región de Murcia. Murcia: Espacio AV, 2009.

Francesca Woodman: Photographs 1975–1980, foreword by Betsy Berne, text by Benjamin H.D. Buchloh. New York: Marian Goodman Gallery, 2004.

Chris Townsend, *Francesca Woodman. Scattered in Space and Time*, texts by Betsy Berne and George Woodman. London: Phaidon, 2006.

Francesca Woodman. Providence, Roma, New York, ed. Rossella Caruso and Cecilia Casorati, texts by Achille Bonito Oliva, Rosella Caruso, Giuseppe Casetti and Cecilia Casorati. Rome: Palazzo delle Esposizioni, Castelvecchi Arte, 2000.

Francesca Woodman, ed. Hervé Chandès, texts by Elizabeth Janus, David Levi Strauss, Sloan Rankin, and Philippe Sollers, Fondation Cartier pour l'art contemporain, Paris. Arles: Actes Sud, 1998.

Francesca Woodman. Photographische Arbeiten / Photographic Works, texts by Harm Lux and Kathryn Hixson. Zurich: Shedhalle/Münster: Westfälischer Kunstverein, 1992.

Francesca Woodman. Photographic Work, ed. Ann Gabhart, texts by Ann Gabhart, Rosalind Krauss, and Abigail Solomon-Godeau. New York: Wellesley College Museum and Hunter College Art Gallery, 1986.

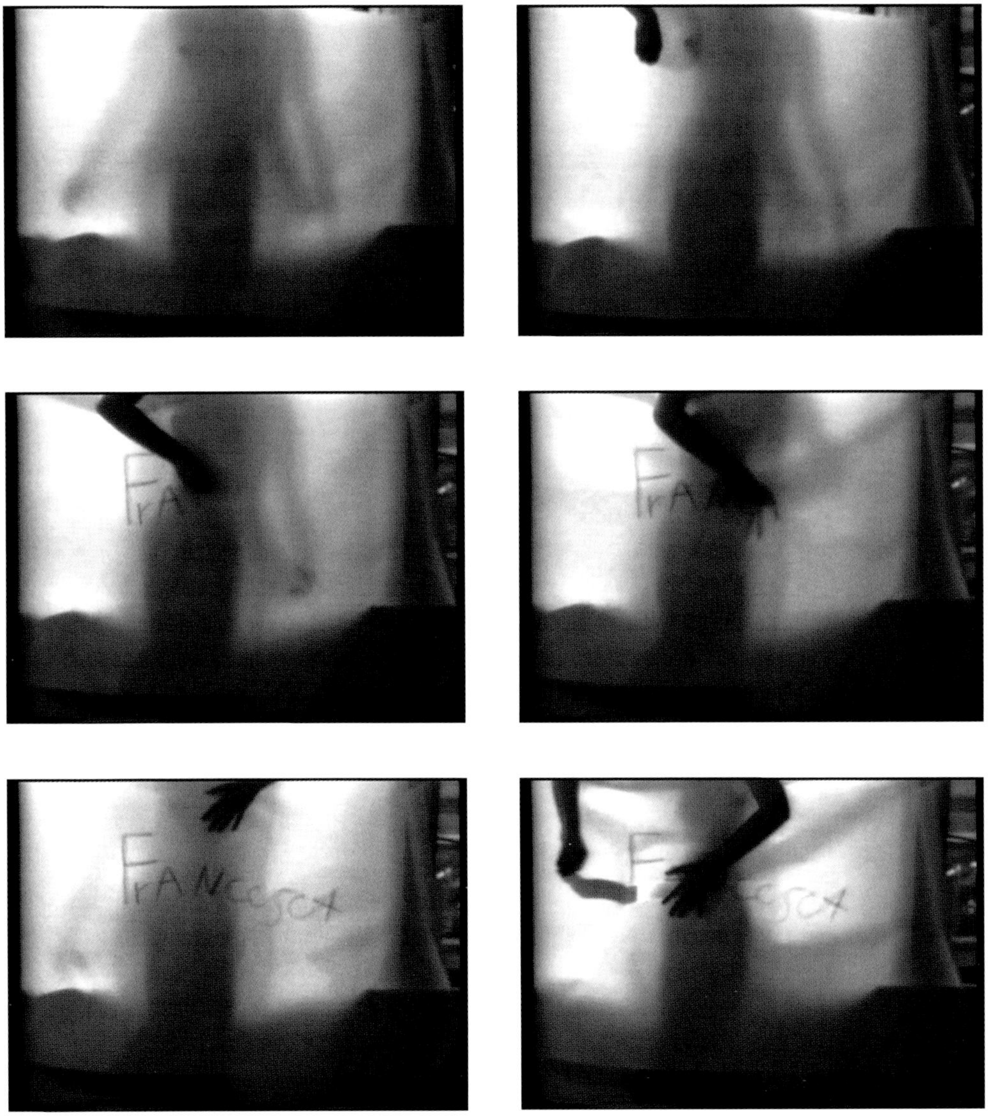

Selected Video Works, Providence, Rhode Island, 1976–78

List of Works

All photographs in the exhibition have been loaned by George and Betty Woodman, The Estate of Francesca Woodman, New York. They are Estate prints, printed in New York from 2000 to 2015. The photographs were matted and framed at Moderna Museet in Stockholm.

Self-portrait at thirteen, Antella, Italy, 1972
Gelatin silver print
17.2 × 16.8 cm
p. 36

Untitled, Boulder, Colorado, 1972–75
Gelatin silver print
16.3 × 10.6 cm
p. 39

Untitled, Providence, Rhode Island, 1975–78
Gelatin silver print
15.4 × 16.6 cm
p. 51

Untitled, Providence, Rhode Island, 1975–76
Gelatin silver print
14.3 × 14.2 cm
p. 52

Untitled, Providence, Rhode Island, 1975–78
Gelatin silver print
13.6 × 13.8 cm
p. 73

Untitled, Providence, Rhode Island, 1975–78
Gelatin silver print
13.8 × 13.5 cm
p. 110

Untitled, Providence, Rhode Island, 1975–78
Gelatin silver print
12.7 × 12.8 cm
p. 127

On Being an Angel, Providence, Rhode Island, 1976
Gelatin silver print
13.3 × 13.5 cm
p. 33

Easter Lilies, Providence, Rhode Island, 1976
Gelatin silver print
11.7 × 11.4 cm
p. 41

Space², Providence, Rhode Island, 1976
Gelatin silver print
13.2 × 13.5 cm
p. 43

Space², Providence, Rhode Island, 1976
Gelatin silver print
13 × 12.1 cm
p. 44

Space^2*,* Providence, Rhode Island, 1976
Gelatin silver print
13.5 × 13.5 cm
p. 45

Space^2*,* Providence, Rhode Island, 1976
Gelatin silver print
13.4 × 12.7 cm
p. 47

From Space^2*,* Providence, Rhode Island, 1976
Gelatin silver print
12.9 × 12.7 cm
p. 48

House #3, Providence, Rhode Island, 1976
Gelatin silver print
16.2 × 16.3 cm
p. 55

House #4, Providence, Rhode Island, 1976
Gelatin silver print
14.4 × 14.5 cm
p. 57

House #4, Providence, Rhode Island, 1976
Gelatin silver print
13.6 × 13.6 cm
p. 59

From Space^2*,* Providence, Rhode Island, 1976
Gelatin silver print
16.2 × 16.2 cm
p. 60

Polka Dots, Providence, Rhode Island, 1976
Gelatin silver print
13.4 × 13.4 cm
p. 63

Polka Dots #5, Providence, Rhode Island, 1976
Gelatin silver print
13.5 × 13.5 cm
p. 65

Polka Dots, Providence, Rhode Island, 1976
Gelatin silver print
11.9 × 9.8 cm
p. 67

From Polka Dots, Providence, Rhode Island, 1976
Gelatin silver print
13 × 13 cm
p. 69

Lightning Legs, Providence, Rhode Island, 1976
Gelatin silver print
13 × 13.1 cm
p. 70

Verticale, Providence, Rhode Island, 1976
Gelatin silver print
12.4 × 12.5 cm
p. 85

Horizontale, Providence, Rhode Island, 1976
Gelatin silver print
13.3 × 12.4 cm
p. 86

From the three kinds of melon in four kinds of light series, Providence, Rhode Island, 1976
Gelatin silver print
12.5×10.1 cm
p. 89

Untitled, Boulder, Colorado, 1976
Gelatin silver print
12.1×12 cm
p. 91

Face, Providence, Rhode Island, 1976
Gelatin silver print
12.3×12.4 cm
p. 92

Untitled, Providence, Rhode Island, 1976
Gelatin silver print
11.8×12.1 cm
p. 95

Untitled, Providence, Rhode Island, 1976
Gelatin silver print
12.4×12 cm
p. 97

Then at one point I did not need to translate the notes; they went directly to my hands, Providence, Rhode Island, 1976
Gelatin silver print
14×14 cm
p. 113

And I had forgotten how to read music, Providence, Rhode Island, 1976
Gelatin silver print
10.9×10.9 cm
p. 117

Untitled, Providence, Rhode Island, 1976
Gelatin silver print
14.4×14.4 cm
p. 147

Untitled, Providence, Rhode Island, 1976
Gelatin silver print
14×14 cm
p. 148

About Being My Model, Providence, Rhode Island, 1976
Gelatin silver print
13.5×13.6 cm
p. 149

Spring in Providence #1, Providence, Rhode Island, 1976
Gelatin silver print
17.1×16.4 cm
p. 151

Spring in Providence #2, Providence, Rhode Island, 1976
Gelatin silver print
16.4×16.9 cm
p. 153

Spring in Providence #3, Providence, Rhode Island, 1976
Gelatin silver print
16.6×16.8 cm
p. 154

Spring in Providence #4, Providence, Rhode Island, 1976
Gelatin silver print
16.3×16.1 cm
p. 155

Charlie the Model #3, Providence, Rhode Island, 1976–77
Gelatin silver print
12.8 × 13.8 cm
p. 98

Charlie the Model #4, Providence, Rhode Island, 1976–77
Gelatin silver print
14.1 × 13.8 cm
p. 99

Charlie the Model #5, Providence, Rhode Island, 1976–77
Gelatin silver print
12.5 × 12.7 cm
p. 101

Charlie the Model #6, Providence, Rhode Island, 1976–77
Gelatin silver print
12.4 × 12.4 cm
p. 103

Charlie the Model #7, Providence, Rhode Island, 1976–77
Gelatin silver print
12.5 × 12.5 cm
p. 104

Charlie the Model #8, Providence, Rhode Island, 1976–77
Gelatin silver print
13.1 × 13.4 cm
p. 105

Charlie the Model #9, Providence, Rhode Island, 1976–77
Gelatin silver print
13.3 × 13 cm
p. 107

Charlie the Model #11, Providence, Rhode Island, 1976–77
Gelatin silver print
14.1 × 14.1 cm
p. 109

Selected Video Works, Providence, Rhode Island, 1976–78
½" open-reel video with sound transferred to DVD, 11:43 min
p. 220

From Angel series, Rome, Italy, 1977
Gelatin silver print
8 × 8.2 cm
p. 25

From a series on Angels, Rome, Italy, 1977
Gelatin silver print
7.9 × 7.8 cm
p. 29

On Being an Angel #1, Providence, Rhode Island, 1977
Gelatin silver print
14.2 × 14.2 cm
p. 35

I could no longer play I could not play by instinct, Providence, Rhode Island, 1977
Gelatin silver print
14.5 × 14.4 cm
p. 115

Self-portrait talking to Vince, Providence, Rhode Island, 1977
Gelatin silver print
13.2 × 13.1 cm
p. 121

Angels, Italy, 1977–78
Gelatin silver print
11.9 × 12 cm
p. 26

Splatter Paint, Rome, Italy, 1977–78
Gelatin silver print
11.7 × 11.7 cm
p. 27

Angels, Italy, 1977–78
Gelatin silver print
9.6 × 9.6 cm
p. 31

Untitled, Rome, Italy, 1977–78
Gelatin silver print
11.7 × 12 cm
p. 125

Untitled, Rome, Italy, 1977–78
Gelatin silver print
20.3 × 20.5 cm
p. 139

Untitled, Rome, Italy, 1977–78
Gelatin silver print
15.1 × 14.9 cm
p. 141

Untitled, Rome, Italy, 1977–78
Gelatin silver print
10.3 × 10.3 cm
p. 143

Untitled, Rome, Italy, 1977–78
Gelatin silver print
11.1 × 11.1 cm
p. 145

From Eel series, Venice, Italy, 1978
Gelatin silver print
15 × 14.8 cm
p. 119

Self-deceit #1, Rome, Italy, 1978
Gelatin silver print
8.8 × 8.7 cm
p. 129

Self-deceit #2, Rome, Italy, 1978
Gelatin silver print
9.1 × 8.6 cm
p. 131

Self-deceit #3, Rome, Italy, 1978
Gelatin silver print
8.5 × 8.7 cm
p. 132

Self-deceit #4, Rome, Italy, 1978
Gelatin silver print
9.2 × 9.4 cm
p. 133

Self-deceit #5, Rome, Italy, 1978
Gelatin silver print
8.9 × 8.6 cm
p. 134

Self-deceit #6, Rome, Italy, 1978
Gelatin silver print
9.1 × 9.1 cm
p. 135

Self-deceit #7, Rome, Italy, 1978
Gelatin silver print
11 × 11.4 cm
p. 137

Untitled (from Swan Song series), Providence, Rhode Island, 1978
Digitally exposed chromogenic print
87 × 102.9 cm
p. 187

Untitled (from Swan Song series), Providence, Rhode Island, 1978
Digitally exposed chromogenic print
99.7 × 94 cm
p. 189

Untitled (from Swan Song series), Providence, Rhode Island, 1978
Digitally exposed chromogenic print
89.5 × 83.8 cm
p. 191

Untitled (from Swan Song series), Providence, Rhode Island, 1978
Digitally exposed chromogenic print
94.6 × 97.2 cm
p. 192

Untitled, New York, 1979
Digitally exposed chromogenic print
8.5 × 8.8 cm
p. 157

Untitled, New York, 1979
Digitally exposed chromogenic print
8.4 × 8.8 cm
p. 159

Untitled, New York, 1979
Digitally exposed chromogenic print
8.5 × 8.5 cm
p. 160

Untitled, New York, 1979
Digitally exposed chromogenic print
8.5 × 8.9 cm
p. 161

Untitled, New York, 1979
Digitally exposed chromogenic print
8.5 × 8.9 cm
p. 162

Untitled, New York, 1979
Digitally exposed chromogenic print
8.5 × 8.8 cm
p. 163

Untitled, New York, 1979
Digitally exposed chromogenic print
8.5 × 8.8 cm
p. 164

Untitled, New York, 1979–80
Gelatin silver print
14.8 × 14.6 cm
p. 81

Untitled, New York, 1979–80
Gelatin silver print
15.3 × 15.3 cm
p. 82

Untitled, New York, 1979–80
Gelatin silver print
13.5 × 13.3 cm
p. 122

Untitled, New York, 1979–80
Gelatin silver print
13.4 × 13.7 cm
p. 123

Untitled, New York, 1979–80
Digitally exposed chromogenic print
8.5 × 8.8 cm
p. 165

Untitled, New York, 1979–80
Gelatin silver print
15.4 × 15.4 cm
p. 167

Untitled, MacDowell/Stanwood, 1979–80
Gelatin silver print
10.9 × 14.9 cm
p. 169

Untitled, New York, 1979–80
Gelatin silver print
13.4 × 13.4
p. 171

Untitled, New York, 1979–80
Gelatin silver print
10 × 24.1 cm
p. 173

Untitled, New York, 1979–80
Gelatin silver print
12.6 × 12.6 cm
p. 175

Untitled, New York, 1979–80
Gelatin silver print
21.7 × 21.4 cm
p. 177

But lately I find a sliver of mirror is simply to slice an eyelid, New York, 1979–80
Gelatin silver print
13.8 × 13.8 cm
p. 179

Untitled, New York, 1979–80
Gelatin silver print
10 × 14.3 cm
p. 181

Untitled, New York, 1979–80
Gelatin silver print
24.1 × 31.1 cm
p. 183

Untitled, MacDowell Colony,
Peterborough, New Hampshire, 1980
Gelatin silver print
27.9 × 35.6 cm
pp. 74–75

Untitled, MacDowell Colony,
Peterborough, New Hampshire, 1980
Gelatin silver print
10.4 × 9.6 cm
p. 77

Untitled, MacDowell Colony,
Peterborough, New Hampshire, 1980
Gelatin silver print
11.4 × 11.3 cm
p. 79

Untitled, MacDowell Colony,
Peterborough, New Hampshire, 1980
Gelatin silver print
23.6 × 20.2 cm
p. 185

Caryatid (study for Temple Project),
New York, 1980
Pigment-based inkjet print from the
original diazotype
201 × 92 cm
p. 195

Caryatid, New York, 1980
Pigment-based inkjet print from the
original diazotype
252.7 × 92 cm
p. 197

Caryatid, New York, 1980
Pigment-based inkjet print from the
original diazotype
181 × 92 cm
p. 199

Zig Zag Study, New York, 1980
Pigment-based inkjet print from the
original diazotype
36.2 × 191.8 cm
pp. 200–201

Head on Rug, New York, 1980
Pigment-based inkjet print from the
original diazotype
92.7 × 317.5 cm
pp. 202–203

Authors

Anna-Karin Palm is a Swedish author. Her first novel, *Faunen* (The Faun), from 1991, was very well received by both reviewers and the reading public, and in 1997 Palm had her breakthrough with the novel *Målarens döttrar* (The Painter's Daughters), which became a bestseller in Sweden and was translated into several languages. She has published numerous titles over the years. Her most recent novel, *Jaktlycka* (The Thrill of the Hunt), from 2014, is a collection of short stories set around the female body, describing women from the age of 16 to 80, different stages of life and different physical experiences.

Anna Tellgren, PhD, has been Curator of Photography at Moderna Museet since 2004. Previously, she has worked as a researcher and as a teacher at the Department of Art History at Stockholm University. As a curator, she has produced exhibitions such as *Arbus, Model, Strömholm* (2005), *Lars Tunbjörk. Winter/Home* (2007), *Moderna Museet Now: Inta Ruka* (2008), and in 2011 she was responsible for the project *Another Story. Photography from the Moderna Museet Collection*, a major presentation of photography throughout the entire museum. She was the editor of *The History Book. On Moderna Museet 1958–2008* (2008) and is associate editor of *Konsthistorisk tidskrift/Journal of Art History*.

George Woodman is a photographer and painter whose exhibitions include *19 Americans*, Guggenheim Museum, New York, 1981; *Pitti Rivisitato: Fotographie di George Woodman*, Palazzo Pitti, Florence, 1997; *Imagenes de Tiempo, Sensibilidad y Sombra*, Museo del Chopo, Mexico City, 1999; *Photographs of George Woodman*, Amethyst Gallery, Chennai, India, 2002, and Galleria Bagnai in Florence in 2010 and 2012. His work is in the permanent collections of The Museum of Modern Art, The Guggenheim Museum, and The Whitney Museum of American Art, among others. He is Professor Emeritus at the University of Colorado in Boulder. Woodman lives half of each year in New York and in Antella, Italy.

This catalog has been published in conjunction with the exhibition
Francesca Woodman. On Being an Angel

Organized and produced by Moderna Museet, Stockholm

Moderna Museet, Stockholm
September 5–December 6, 2015

Foam Photography Museum, Amsterdam
December 18, 2015–March 9, 2016

Fondation Henri Cartier-Bresson, Paris
May 11–July 31, 2016

Moderna Museet Malmö
November 5, 2016–March 19, 2017

The Finnish Museum of Photography, Helsinki
August 24–October 15, 2017

Fundación Canal, Madrid
October 3, 2019–January 5, 2020

C/O Berlin Foundation, Berlin
March 7–September 5, 2020

Exhibition
Curator: Anna Tellgren
Exhibition coordinator: Desirée Blomberg
Curator programme: Karin Malmquist
Photography conservator: Teresa Mesquit
Head of technicians: Harry Nahkala
Exhibition architect: Ann Bexelius

Catalogue
Editor: Anna Tellgren
Managing editor: Teresa Hahr
Translation: Saskia Vogel
Proofreader: Danko Szabó
Prepress: Albin Dahlström
Graphic design: Patric Leo
Printing: Printer Trento via Italgraf Media 2024, 5th edition

Moderna Museet exhibition catalog no. 387
ISBN 978-91-86243-70-8 (Moderna Museet)
ISBN 978-3-86335-750-4 (Verlag der Buchhandlung
Walther und Franz König)

www.modernamuseet.se

Cover: *On Being an Angel #1*, Providence, Rhode Island, 1977

Published by Moderna Museet,
Stockholm and Verlag der Buchhandlung
Walther und Franz König, Köln

Distribution:
Buchhandlung Walther König
Ehrenstr. 4
D-50672 Cologne
Tel: +49 (0) 221 / 20 59 6 53
verlag@buchhandlung-walther-koenig.de
www.buchhandlung-walther-koenig.de